Apache Tactics 1830–86

ROBERT N. WATT

ILLUSTRATED BY ADAM HOOK
Series editor Martin Windrow

First published in Great Britain in 2012 by Osprey Publishing,
Midland House, West Way, Botley, Oxford, OX2 0PH, UK
44-02 23rd Street, Suite 219, Long Island City, NY 11101, USA
E-mail: info@ospreypublishing.com

OSPREY PUBLISHING IS PART OF THE OSPREY GROUP

A CIP catalog record for this book is available from the British Library

Print ISBN: 978 1 84908 630 1
PDF ebook ISBN: 978 1 84908 631 8
ePub ebook ISBN: 978 1 78096 031 9

Editor: Martin Windrow
Page layout by Ken Vail Graphic Design, Cambridge, UK (kvgd.com)
Index by Fineline Editorial Services
Typeset in Sabon and Myriad Pro
Originated by Blenheim Colour Ltd, Oxford
Printed in China through Worldprint Ltd

12 13 14 15 16 17 10 9 8 7 6 5 4 3 2 1

Osprey Publishing is supporting the Woodland Trust, the UK's leading
woodland conservation charity, by funding the dedication of trees.

www.ospreypublishing.com

ACKNOWLEDGMENTS

The author would like to thank the following for their help and
encouragement: Catherine Edwards, Willy Dobak, Dan Aranda, Emilio Tapia,
Berndt Kuhn, Ed Sweeney, Bill Cavaliere, Eric and Kathy Fuller, Spike
Flanders, Frank Brito, Mary Williams, Karl Laumbach, Chris Adams, Ron
Burkett, James Irby, Allan Redbourne, Robert Wooster, Durwood Ball, Diana
Hadley and Martin Windrow.

ARTIST'S NOTE

Readers may care to note that the original paintings from which the color
plates in this book were prepared are available for private sale. All
reproduction copyright whatsoever is retained by the Publishers. All
enquiries should be addressed to:

Scorpio Gallery, PO Box 475, Hailsham, East Sussex BN27 2SL, UK

The Publishers regret that they can enter into no correspondence upon this
matter.

Front cover: Geronimo (left) and Naiche (right) on horseback,
photographed during their negotiations with General Crook at Canyon de
los Embudos in March 1886. (Photo C.S. Fly; courtesy Arizona Historical
Society, no. 78163)

Title page: A faded but interesting photo of a US Army officer with a group
of Apache scouts. One of the latter wears a US Army M1872 dress helmet,
and the officer has adopted a non-regulation hat and fringed leggings.
(Courtesy Arizona Historical Society, no. 19841)

CONTENTS

APACHE TACTICS 1830–86

INTRODUCTION

In the middle to late 19th century, Apaches often out-fought their Mexican and American opponents by deploying a wide range of skilfully developed guerrilla strategies and tactics. By 1876 Apache guerrillas had adopted, through trade and capture, modern breech-loading rifles, which allowed them to develop a more aggressive style of warfare than their earlier hit-and-run tactics, which had been limited by the use of bows and muzzle-loading muskets. During the 1870s and 1880s their guerrilla skills proved so effective that the US Army ultimately had to "become Apaches" in order to defeat them, relying heavily on large numbers of Apaches enrolled in the companies of Indian Scouts.

During the 17th and 18th centuries the Spanish colonists of Mexico and the old Southwest had variable success against the Apaches. Their policies veered back and forth, between outright extermination by the use of military force, and attempted assimilation by the use of the *presidio* system – the establishment of scattered centers that combined the characteristics of colonial forts, Catholic missions and civil settlements. It was argued that this system, though expensive, would gradually undermine the Apaches' ability to resist: attracted to settle around these sources of food and trade goods, they would become so dependent upon such resources that they would lose their ability to survive independently. The goods supplied to them included not only beef and alcohol, but also sub-standard muskets, which only the Spanish would be able to repair for them.

In the later 18th century the Spanish combined this approach with pressure to "assimilate, or be exterminated," which, although not wholly successful, did produce a period of relative peace in the early 19th century. However, this did not long survive Mexico's achievement of independence from Spain in 1821. By the 1830s the Mexicans were unable or unwilling to continue funding and administering the *presidio* system, and relations with the Apaches broke down into a relentless cycle of war, temporary truce, and renewed war. The authorities in the Mexican states of Sonora and Chihuahua – with little Federal control, and often sunk in near-anarchic internal rivalries – resorted to offering cash bounties for the scalps of Apache men, women and children. Inevitably, atrocity begat atrocity, and some areas became actually uninhabitable by Mexicans – for example, the mining center of Santa

This posed study of an Apache warrior (whose name is given phonetically as "Goodygouye") is a good deal more convincing than most. It shows a short, muscular man wearing a headband, breechclout and knee-length moccasins – the preferred fighting dress of an Apache. He is armed with a .45/70 Springfield M1873 rifle, and a revolver holstered butt-forwards on his left hip from his cartridge belt. Handguns appear in a number of photos of Apaches, and an account of an action by a detachment from the 9th US Cavalry in 1879 mentions one of their Navajo scouts being killed by a warrior with a revolver. (Courtesy Arizona Historical Society, no. 41255)

Rita near the Pinos Altos Mts, abandoned under the attacks of the Mimbreno Apaches led by the vengeful chief Mangas Coloradas.[1] Nevertheless, at the same time the current governors of each state were capable of reaching temporary truces with the Apaches. The latter often turned this to their

1 For notes on the different Apache tribes and groups, and aspects of Apache culture, see Osprey Men-at-Arms 186, *The Apaches*, by Jason & Richard Hook. The most basic tribal divisions were as follows: *Jicarilla* (Olleros/Hoyeros & Llaneros groups; NE New Mexico & S Colorado); *Mescalero* (Sacramento, Guadelupe & Davis Mts of SE New Mexico, & W Texas); *Chiricahua* (Eastern – Mimbreno & Warm Springs groups, SW New Mexico; Central – Chokonen or "Cochise" group, SE Arizona, New Mexico & Mexico; Southern – Nednhi or "Bronco," Sierra Madre Mts of Mexico); and *Western Apaches* (White Mountain/Coyotero, Cibecue, San Carlos, N & S Tonto groups, Arizona)

advantage: if they were at peace with Sonora, they would raid in Chihuahua and trade their plunder back in Sonora, and vice versa.

The regional authorities of the United States became embroiled in this situation after the USA annexed a huge segment of Mexican territory following victory in the Mexican-American War (1846–48). The Apaches took similar advantage of the international frontier as they did of regional borders, and the cycle of "trade/hate" relations continued until Geronimo's surrender in September 1886. (As Geronimo was being escorted out of Mexico during that month by Apache scouts and US troops, a large body of Mexican troops shadowed them. Much to the US officers' consternation, their Indian Scouts prepared for a fight, and Geronimo made it known that he and his warriors would side with the Americans if the Mexicans attacked. Hostilities were avoided only after a tense round of negotiation between the US and Mexican officers.)

There were a number of violent incidents between Americans and Apaches in the 1840s and 1850s, and an influx of American miners and settlers

In most studio photographs – as here – Apaches are shown wearing their best clothing. This scout also holds a single-shot M1873 Springfield, the most common model of rifle and carbine carried in the later Indian Wars. (Courtesy Arizona Historical Society, no. 50136)

Parts of Apacheria are far from the Hollywood image of arid desert. This scene gives an idea of the dense vegetation that can be found near water or higher in the mountain ranges. (Courtesy Arizona Historical Society, no. 14896)

By contrast, this bleak view shows the buildings at the San Carlos Indian Agency, between the Salt and Gila rivers. The Chiricahuas who were sent to San Carlos in the mid-1870s were settled on the barren and unhealthy land that was not already occupied by the Western Apaches – whom they regarded with suspicion, or outright hostility. (Courtesy Arizona Historical Society, no. 19864)

into New Mexico led to new tensions with the Chiricahua Apaches. Mangas Coloradas was provoked into war by encroachments into his territory and an attack on an Apache camp in December 1860. Early in 1861 his ally Cochise was wrongly accused of raiding and kidnapping, and was held by US troops while under a flag of truce. Cochise managed to break free, but his brother and five other Apache warriors were detained; Cochise in turn took four Americans hostage, and when negotiations broke down both sides killed their prisoners. Between 1860 and 1886, the Apaches would pursue the traditional cycle of alternating war and truce with the USA. The situation was aggravated during the early 1860s by the simultaneous American Civil War, which left regional security in the hands of local volunteers rather than regular Federal troops.

* * *

This book's title refers to the whole period 1830–1886, because the essential nature of Apache strategies and tactics was unchanged throughout that half-century. (In this context "strategy" is used to mean maneuvers undertaken out of sight of the enemy, and "tactics" refers to maneuvers on the battlefield, within sight of the enemy.) Although it largely relies upon illustrative examples from the warfare orchestrated by two of the most able Chiricahua Apache leaders, Victorio (Bi-du-ya) and Nana (Kas-tziden), principally in New Mexico and Chihuahua from 1879 to 1881, incidents from the earlier Apache wars and the period 1882–86 are also mentioned where appropriate.

An essential point to note is the relatively small scale of this type of warfare. This was not war conducted in the grand manner, but a classic "small war," where it was unusual for the total number of fighting men to exceed 3,000 at any one time. The Apaches of the 1830s to 1860s could sometimes mount expeditions involving several hundred warriors, but the long war of attrition with the Mexicans and then the Americans took a steady toll. By the climactic period between 1879 and 1883 Apache leaders rarely directed more than a hundred warriors at a time; yet their tried and tested guerrilla strategies and tactics often left their far more numerous US and Mexican opponents confounded, while the threat that they were believed to present paralyzed economic activity in northern Mexico, Arizona and New Mexico. The last resistance mounted in 1885–86 by Geronimo, Naiche, Nana, Ulzana and his brother Chihuahua (his Mexican name – not to be confused with the Mexican state) involved fewer than 50 warriors. Yet this band was still able to ambush and defeat at least one US Army detachment less than four months before they finally surrendered in 1886. The aim of this book is to give readers an idea of why and how such small numbers of fighting men managed to hold out for so many years before finally succumbing to the vastly greater manpower and firepower of the United States. In the process, it is hoped to suggest wider lessons to be learned from one of modern history's most impressive examples of "classic" guerrilla tactics.

CHRONOLOGY

1821 Mexico gains independence from Spain.
1830s–1850s Intermittent warfare between the Mexicans of Chihuahua and Sonora states and the Apaches is characterized by raid and counter-raid, massacre and retaliation, punctuated by temporary and unreliable truces.

Periodically, both Mexican states resort to uncoordinated policies of extermination, by offering bounties for Apache scalps.

1848 A large tract of "Apacheria" passes into the jurisdiction of the USA at the end of the Mexican-American War.

Dec 1860 An unprovoked attack on an Apache village by a party of miners provokes Mangas Coloradas of the Eastern Chiricahua into war with the Americans.

Feb 1861 A false accusation of raiding and kidnapping, and the mutual killing of hostages, provoke Cochise of the Central Chiricahua into open warfare with the USA, in collaboration with Mangas Coloradas.

1861–62 On the outbreak of the Civil War the few Federal troops based in Arizona depart, and the citizens of the territory find themselves in a state of siege by the Apaches.

1862 As part of an effort to drive Confederate forces out of Arizona and New Mexico, Gen Carleton marches east at the head of volunteer Union troops raised in California. **July 14:** The advance guard is ambushed in Apache Pass by large numbers of Apaches directed by Cochise and Mangas Coloradas. The deployment of two mountain howitzers decides the day for the Californians.

1862–71 A prolonged guerrilla war of attrition ensues between the USA and Apaches led by Cochise and Mangas Coloradas. **Jan 1863:** Mangas Coloradas, taken prisoner under a flag of truce, is shot "while trying to escape." Cochise continues the fight; neither side gains the upper hand, but both US and Mexican forces inflict steady casualties upon the Chiricahuas, which ultimately prove unsustainable. By 1871 Cochise is willing to consider peace overtures. Independently, the Western Apaches, some of whom had allied with Cochise in the early 1860s, continue making periodic raids upon US citizens.

April 1871 Tucson citizens and Papago Indians slaughter peaceful Western Apaches in the "Camp Grant massacre." A national outcry, and continued raids by infuriated Apaches, prompt the appointment of LtCol George Crook as commander of the Department of Arizona. He arrives in June with a remit to force an end to hostilities, while a peace commission under Vincent Colyer and Gen Oliver Howard is sent to establish reservations.

Sept–Oct 1872 Gen Howard concludes a peace treaty with Cochise, who agrees to settle on a reservation based on the Dragoon and Chiricahua Mts around Fort Bowie, Arizona. This brings Cochise's 11-year war with the USA to an end, and saves the Chiricahua from being targeted in Crook's forthcoming "Tonto Basin campaign" against the Western Apaches in Arizona. Other Chiricahua bands at Old Fort Tularosa reservation remain restless, wishing to move to the Ojo Caliente (Warm Springs) reservation in New Mexico.

Nov 1872–April 1873 Crook launches several company-sized columns each accompanied by Indian Scouts, and keeps them in the field for long periods by use of mule-trains.These tactics take the Western Apaches by surprise; they suffer heavy casualties, and the winter campaign destroys their will to resist. Key defeats are inflicted at Salt River Cave in **Dec 1872**, and Turret Mountain in **March 1873**. Most of the Western Apaches agree to settle upon reservations around Fort Apache and San Carlos. Crook is promoted to brigadier-general.

1873–74 Gen Crook keeps his troops and scouts in the field against uncowed Western Apache bands, launching a second offensive in

1

advance guard

left flank guard

right flank guard

rear guard

2

Jan 1874. This inflicts further serious losses, culminating in the killing of the remaining militant leaders by **Aug 1874.** In the same year Cochise dies of natural causes; and the US government agrees to Victorio's people returning to Ojo Caliente.

1875–76 The Department of the Interior adopts a new cost-cutting policy to concentrate all Apaches – of mutually hostile tribes and bands – on a single reservation at San Carlos; this disastrous mistake is largely responsible for the Apache wars of **1877–86.** The Chiricahua reservation around Fort Bowie is closed, and its inhabitants are moved to San Carlos.

1877–79 The concentration policy gathers momentum. **May 1877,** the Ojo Caliente reservation is closed, and Apaches led by Victorio, Loco and Nana are transferred to San Carlos. They protest this move, and in **Sept 1877** they lead warriors in breaking out of the reservation. The US government authorizes Gen Edward Ord, then commanding the Department of Texas, to mount "hot pursuits" over the Mexican border. Between **Oct 1877** and **Aug 1879,** Victorio and Nana fight for a return to Warm Springs; Loco chooses to return to San Carlos and pursue the same goal peacefully.

Sept 1879–May 1880 Having caused minimal casualties in the US between 1877 and 1879, Victorio loses patience, and wages all-out war against the USA and Mexico. He outwits or defeats every force sent against him, and his warriors inflict heavy casualties upon the citizens and soldiers of both countries. He is gradually worn down by a defeat at the hands of Apache scouts in **May 1880,** and by being outmaneuvered by the 10th US Cavalry in West Texas during **July–Aug 1880.**

Oct 1880 Victorio is finally trapped and killed at Tres Castillos by *c.*400 Mexican state troops led by Joaquin Terrazas, supported by a large US expedition that enters Mexico by agreement with state authorities but without permission from the weak Mexican central government.

July–Aug 1881 Nana, Victorio's successor, regroups survivors of Tres Castillos and launches a legendary raid into New Mexico. At the age of about 75 years, he leads his raiders approx. 1,500 miles in six weeks, holds off

Apacheria: a view roughly southwards from the western end of Cooke's Canyon. The Florida Mts are in the middle distance approximately 15 miles away, and the Tres Hermanas Mts are visible on the horizon, about 35 miles off and just short of the Mexican border. Note that the nearer, "level" ground is in fact anything but featureless; it was in this valley that Victorio's warriors laid an ambush from an almost invisible *arroyo* and cut down five men passing on the trail in May 1880. (Author's photo).

A typical Apache camp in scrubby terrain. Such camps were carefully sited to avoid detection, in defensible places with a choice of escape routes; they could be moved quickly and quietly, and sometimes decoy camps were constructed to mislead the enemy. The *wikiup* huts were also widely dispersed so that they could not be overrun quickly, giving most of the women and children a chance to escape from even a successful surprise attack. Captain John Bourke was told by Apache scouts that for the sake of concealment the Chiricahuas did not light cooking fires until after 9am, when the darkness had completely lifted. (Courtesy Arizona Historical Society, no. 62111)

or defeats at least seven US Army detachments, and inflicts heavy casualties among ranching and mining communities in southern New Mexico.

Aug 1881 Western Apache scouts mutiny when the US Army arrests an Apache spiritual leader at Cibecue Creek. This incident provokes Western Apaches – alienated by US government failure to honor treaty obligations undertaken following Crook's campaigns – to make a direct attack upon Fort Apache on **Sept 1, 1881,** but they soon withdraw.

Sept 1881 Alarmed by US Army activity following the Cibecue mutiny and the attack on Fort Apache, Juh and many Chiricahuas flee from the San Carlos reservation into Mexico. They take refuge in the Sierra Madre Mts, and join forces with Nana, recently returned to Mexico from his raid into New Mexico.

April 1882 The Apaches from the Sierra Madre arrive at San Carlos and force Loco and his Warm Springs Apaches to return with them to Mexico. They are pursued by US Cavalry and Apache scouts, and ambushed by Mexican troops. Of the 400 Apaches who leave the reservation, more than 100 are killed before they reach the Sierra Madre.

July 1882 The dissident Western Apaches are finally cornered by US troops and Apache scouts at Big Dry Wash/Chevelon Fork, and the survivors disperse. General Crook, recalled to Arizona in response to the crisis, quickly addresses Western Apache grievances.

May–June 1883 Crook, with a force mainly made up of Apache scouts, penetrates the Chiricahua strongholds in the Sierra Madre Mts. Benefiting from his reputation among the Apaches for honest dealing, he persuades them to surrender.

Feb 1884 Geronimo is the last Chiricahua to arrive from Mexico after the peace agreement with Gen Crook.

May 1885 Geronimo, Naiche, Mangus, Nana, Ulzana and Chihuahua flee the San Carlos reservation.

Nov–Dec 1885 Ulzana leads a small party of warriors into the USA and causes widespread disruption before returning to Mexico.

March 1886 General Crook meets with the Apaches at Canyon de los Embudos. Nana, Ulzana, Chihuahua and their followers surrender, and are sent back to the USA, but Geronimo and Naiche flee. Crook resigns and is replaced by Col Nelson Miles. The surrendered Chiricahua Apaches and those who remained on the reservation are deported to Florida.

Sept–Oct 1886 Geronimo and his followers surrender in Skeleton Canyon; they are deported to Florida – along with those Chiricahuas who had served as scouts. A small separate group led by Mangus returns to the USA to surrender, and is also sent to Florida.

ENVIRONMENT AND CULTURE

Before examining the techniques of Apache warfare, we should note a number of factors that influenced the development of these strategies and tactics. One profound influence was, of course, the natural environment of what is called today "Apacheria"; another was the Apache culture of warrior training, and of leadership gained by merit rather than inheritance.

The popular image of the Apache guerrilla is one of a hardy desert warrior accustomed to surviving in the arid terrain of New Mexico and Arizona. This image is not inaccurate, but it fails to take into account that while the Apaches certainly knew how to survive in this harsh land, they did not choose to live in the desert unless absolutely necessary. All the tribes were essentially hunters and gatherers, completely attuned to the natural world of plant and animal life in even the most apparently barren areas, but some – particularly the Western and Jicarilla Apaches – also practiced agriculture. Apacheria is a region of wide extremes, from high mountain peaks to low-lying deserts, where temperatures ranged from below freezing in winter to 100°F (38°C) in August. If we examine a map of the area, and some of the photos in this book, we can see that the terrain is spotted not only with scorched mesas rising above the flats and canyons, but also with mountain ranges that are often covered in pine forest and have good water. It was in such relatively fertile islands in a desert sea that the Warm Springs (Ojo Caliente) division of the Eastern Chiricahua Apaches chose to live.

The many mountains were also used as landmarks to aid travel between water sources in New Mexico and Chihuahua. When traveling between campsites the Apaches cached extra supplies of dried food, clothing material and ammunition; this practice also helped them to survive if they were surprised by an enemy and forced to abandon their possessions and disperse. Mountain ranges also provided lookout posts. For example, in September 1880 the commandant of Fort Bliss, Capt Brinkerhoff, received intelligence from his own scouts that they had discovered tracks indicating that Victorio had sent small parties to the top of the Potrillo Mountains. From this vantage point the Apaches could detect any movement by the troops concentrated at Fort Cummings southwards into Mexico towards Victorio's camp near the Laguna de Guzman. The distance between the fort and the lagoon is approximately 75 miles (120km), yet lookouts stationed on the Potrillo Mts would have been able to scan much of the distance between these two points.

The locations of camps were carefully chosen, usually upon higher ground with a good view of the surrounding area. US Army officers and scouts in the 1860s and 1870s gave credit to Victorio for his careful selection of camps in difficult terrain. If necessary, the Apaches would often construct small rock breastworks where the terrain did not provide natural cover.

View eastwards from the top of Emory Pass in the southern Black Range (Mimbres Mts), showing the thick pine forest that can be found in the highest ranges. In the dry, clear air one can see long distances from such crests. The mountains on the furthest horizon are the San Andres, some 70 miles distant; those sloping slightly down from left to right on the nearer horizon are the Caballo Mts (see map, Plate C). In January 1880, Maj Morrow's pursuit of Victorio passed from right to left in the middle distance, through the foothills of the Black Range. (Author's photo)

The animals that are found in New Mexico and Chihuahua also influenced the manner in which the Apaches engaged their enemies. While night-fighting was not unknown, they did not like to fight in darkness. The Apaches themselves reported to ethnologists that they feared the ghosts or evil spirits who walked the night, but it is equally plausible that these beliefs were fostered to warn future generations that to fight at night increased the risks of encountering venomous creatures when they were at their most active. The Southwest is a home to tarantulas, Black Widow and Recluse spiders, venomous centipedes and scorpions. There is also a poisonous lizard called the Gila Monster and, last but certainly not least, the Western Diamondback rattlesnake. (An equally practical reason for not fighting at night was, of course, to prevent the wasting of precious ammunition.)

Culture

What any historian has to bear in mind when studying the Apaches is that, from a Euro-American point of view, we are confronted by a very different culture. Two examples should suffice to give the reader an appreciation of Apache views on the role of warfare in their society. A key anthropological work on the Apaches, Opler's *An Apache Life-Way* (see "Further Reading"), reports in great detail their raiding and warfare practices – but in a chapter headed simply but significantly "Maintenance of the Household." Again, when the US authorities proceeded to close the Chiricahua reservation in 1876, a dispute arose amongst Chiricahua Apaches as to whether to accept removal or raise armed resistance. When this debate could not be resolved, it was the "peace faction" that gunned down the "war faction."

To understand Apache warriors, we have to grasp how central hunting, raiding and warfare were to their culture, and how this shaped their response to any perceived threat – be it from other Apaches, other American Indians, Spaniards, Mexicans, or Americans. Apache thinking was focused upon the hunting and fighting skills that were critical to their survival; however, they drew a sharp distinction between raiding to capture property, and war to inflict deaths on an enemy.

Training and leadership

The basic principle of Apache warfare – as among any people with a relatively small and dispersed population – was to inflict maximum damage upon their enemy while sustaining the minimum of losses. To fit them for life in a harsh environment, Apache boys were raised from an early age in such a way as to maximize strength, stamina, and discipline. Such training started young; it included bathing in icy mountain streams, and running long distances in rough terrain – it is well documented that a warrior could run up to 70 miles in a day, and Apache women could achieve very nearly the same distances. Boys were made to run up and down hills with a mouthful of water that was not to be swallowed, to teach them both self-discipline and breath control. Instruction in hunting had the natural consequence of teaching the concealment skills and fieldcraft for which the Apaches were famous. This training ended only once the adolescent boy had successfully completed four raids as an apprentice warrior.

Apache culture extolled individuals who were not only tough but also patient, and successful raiders were those who did not take unnecessary risks. While an element of hereditary succession was not unknown, Apache leadership was based upon merit derived from an individual's record of repeated successful application of these principles. Apache leaders who were perceived to be unsuccessful, particularly if they sustained what were judged to be unnecessary casualties, soon lost their influence. This respect for proven skills explains why Apaches were often found being led by men in their fifties and beyond.

Victorio was believed to be about 50 years old when he was killed at Tres Castillos in 1880, and his lieutenant, Nana, was at least 75 when he led his famous raid into New Mexico the following year. Other Apache leaders of the time such as Juh, Chihuahua and Ulzana (also known as Jolsanny/Josanie) are believed to have been still active in their sixties and seventies. Younger men, such as Kaytennae, only rose to precocious leadership in their twenties by dint of their proven success.

Apache training produced not only excellent leaders, but also warriors who – even if they did not rise to the leadership of large numbers of men – could be trusted to act independently, since they knew exactly what was expected of them. Apaches often operated in separated groups under the broad direction of their chosen leader; this required warriors who could be trusted to act as directed without being directly supervised. Apache warriors tended to group together, in the first instance, according to their closest kinship links, and thus a man could rise to the leadership of his immediate family. If seen as particularly successful, he could gain the allegiance of a number of

Some of the venomous wildlife commonly found in Apacheria: a Western Diamondback rattlesnake, a tarantula, and a scorpion – only visible against the pale ground by its shadow (the rule of thumb is that the smaller their pincers, the more dangerous their sting). While most active at night, such animals may easily be encountered by day – whether by men seeking cover in the 1870s, or by those exploring a historic battle site today. The records of the 6th US Cavalry mention losing a number of horses to rattlesnake bites. (Author's photos)

kinship groups, and eventually he might even attract followers from other tribes. Nevertheless, even highly successful leaders required the presence of this network of individual "family" leaders if they were to implement their strategy and tactics. What we would call "squad leaders" were an essential component of Apache warfare, often being relied upon to make individual judgments as to whether to continue a fight or to withdraw in response to rapidly changing circumstances.

GUERRILLA STRATEGIES & TACTICS

THE RAID

Much of the Apaches' warfare against the Mexicans and Americans from the 1830s to 1886 involved raids aimed at gathering loot that could be consumed, or traded for essential supplies. Captured horses and cattle might be either kept or traded, depending upon circumstances. Guns and ammunition might be captured by raiding, but were more often acquired in exchange for other goods taken in raids.

This Apache, stripped down for action, would have been trained from early boyhood not only to survive in the harsh natural environment, but to thrive in it, and to move across it with a speed, stealth and stamina far beyond those of the Mexican and American soldiers hunting him. He could run and climb for many miles between dawn and sunset in all weathers, finding water and wild food as he went, and during a forced march he might go without sleep for several days. (Courtesy Arizona Historical Society, no. 50132)

While Apache raiding activities sometimes caused the Americans serious problems, it was the Mexicans of northern Sonora and Chihuahua states who sustained the heaviest losses in property and lives. As mentioned above, the Apaches defined raiding as taking property from an enemy, whereas warfare was to take lives. Thus, if Mexican villagers did manage to defend themselves successfully and killed, wounded or captured any Apaches, they would find themselves subject to further attacks inspired by vengeance for previous losses. Between 1883 and 1886, US Army officers serving in northern Mexico in pursuit of Chiricahua Apaches noted the ruins of Mexican settlements often long abandoned. However, this was not usually the result of direct assaults upon villages or *haciendas* (ranches), but of the cumulative effects of relentless hit-and-run attacks. These made it impossible for such small communities to sustain themselves without running a high risk of being picked off by hostile Apaches as they worked in the fields or on the cattle ranges, or made necessary journeys. In time, large areas of northern Sonora were effectively depopulated by these methods.

Where occasional ranches or houses were actually overrun it is unclear how the Apaches accomplished such destruction, since they seldom left survivors to tell the tale. Nevertheless, there are a number of clues as to how the Apaches might storm a building with minimal loss. They would usually mount a careful and patient reconnaissance of the target before risking a direct attack on any building. The most common technique would be to

A posed portrait of a Chiricahua named Ze-Le and his wife; the carbine seems to be a photographer's prop. The Apaches made great use of trade cloth, and at least one supply-cache containing bolts of calico was discovered during military operations in New Mexico. (Courtesy Arizona Historical Society, no. 50134)

employ their legendary stealth of movement to reach the building undetected, and burst in on unsuspecting victims. If there was enough flammable material all they needed to do was to creep close enough to set the building alight, and kill the occupants as they broke out. Apaches could also approach buildings professing friendship and then open fire from point-blank range. Finally, there were occasions where Apaches would stealthily approach a building and fire shots through the doors and windows to test the level of resistance before deciding whether to close in or withdraw. Once the Apaches had access to breech-loading weapons they could change their positions while keeping up a rapid fire, in an attempt to panic the defenders into fleeing the building.

In truth, direct assaults on buildings were very rare, because of the high risk of sustaining unacceptably high casualties. Accounts of Apache attacks upon settlements in northern Mexico fall into two categories. The first were raids aimed at stealing horses or cattle, where any casualties inflicted were incidental to that primary goal. The second were when Apaches were looking to inflict casualties in revenge for previous losses, but their approach was usually detected before they could strike an effective blow. In both cases there

would be enough Mexican survivors to leave a record of their experiences. If an alerted populace managed to reach solid and relatively non-flammable buildings, they would normally be safe from the Apaches until the next attack. The richer Mexican ranchers in the area built their ranches with defenses designed to frustrate Apache raiding, and the photos above show a surviving example of a fairly massive complex with stables and living quarters built in an easily defensible hollow square.

Apache raiding would often provoke a reaction from the Mexicans and Americans, and the Apaches developed a number of responses. These can be divided broadly into evasion, ambush, and attack, and this text is arranged to consider them in turn.

EVASION

One of the greatest challenges when attempting to counter Apache guerrillas was intercepting them in the first place. The Apaches used a number of tricks to coordinate their own movements and evade enemy activity. For signaling between parties they used mirrors during the day and fires at night. When moving from one area to another they put out advance scouts, flanking scouts and rearguards to prevent their being surprised (see Plate A). It would be routine for a rendezvous point to be decided each day in advance of leaving

B **FROM EVASION TO AMBUSH**
Another hypothetical scenario, here from the 1860s, imagines the interception by Mexican *Rurales* (**1, and inset 1**) of a White Mountain Apache raiding party traveling home with stolen cattle. The Mexicans' approach is detected by the left flank guard (**2**), who raise the alarm. When an Apache party were intercepted they might often choose to scatter, and rendezvous later at a pre-arranged location; but on this occasion, with the cattle to protect, they attempt to draw their pursuers into an ambush. At the first alarm the left flank guard join the main body (**3**), and helps screen its retreat towards a

pass in the mountains. The advance guard (**4**) and right flank guard (**5**) race ahead of the main body to reach a suitable spot to spring an ambush once the main body has passed, doubling back across high ground to get into position (**6, and inset 2**). Armed at this date with muzzle-loading weapons or bows and arrows, they find firing positions as close to the trail as possible, but their skill at concealment in even moderate cover is legendary. The rear guard (**7**) confuse the pursuers by taking a different route, but then head for the nearer flank of the defile chosen for the ambush (**8**), to bring the pursuers under fire from both sides.

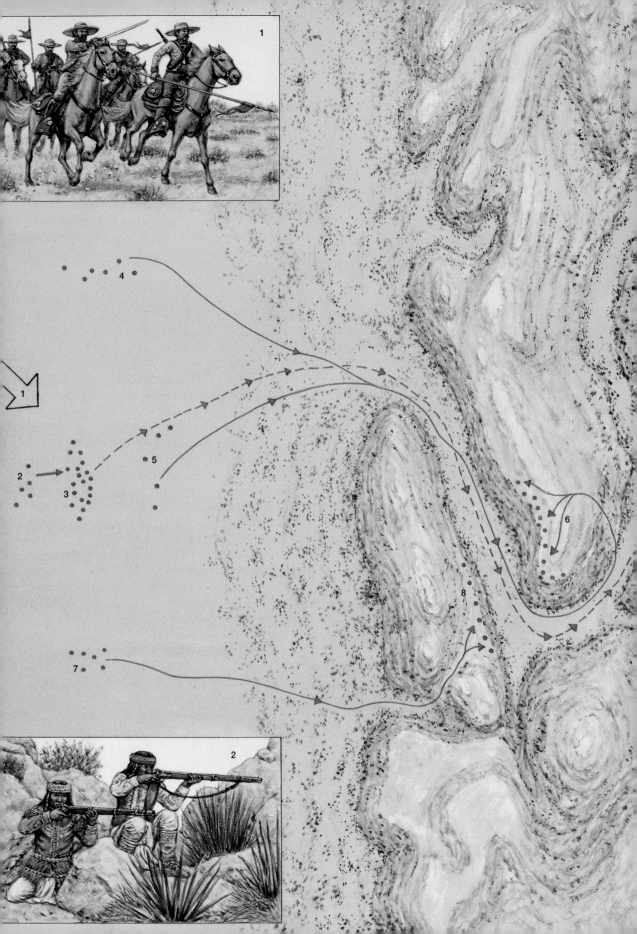

1

2

their camp; the standard response to the appearance of an enemy force was to scatter in order to break contact, and to re-group later at this rendezvous point. Equally, however, if the terrain favored such tactics, then the Apaches might give the appearance of fleeing while in reality leading their pursuers into an ambush (see Plate B). This inclination to evade their enemies unless the conditions for fighting were very favorable proved to be a major headache for the US Army. A deeply frustrated Gen Philip Sheridan noted on October 22, 1879 that:

> their tactics being to attack and plunder some given point, then to scatter like quails and meet again at some other distant point previously understood, for plunder and again scatter [sic], therefore it is exceedingly difficult for our troops to over-take and punish them.

This technique figures in reports from every level of command in the US Army. The Apaches would usually attempt to scatter whether or not their pursuers had spotted them; on at least one occasion they fired dry grass and scrub to hinder the pursuit. However, they would sometimes fight a rearguard action, buying time to allow for the escape of their dependants or of warriors driving stolen livestock.

On August 16, 1881, Lts G. Valois and G.R. Burnett with a small detachment from Company I of the African-American 9th US Cavalry were halted near Canada Alamosa, New Mexico, as one of a number of detachments from that regiment charged with intercepting Apache raiders led by Nana. They were watering their horses at the Rio Alamosa when they received a report that the Chavez ranch downstream had been attacked. Lieutenant Burnett left immediately with a few men, while Lt Valois mustered the rest of the detachment and followed. Arriving at the ranch, Burnett joined forces with a posse of Mexicans intent on avenging those recently killed by the Apaches. As this force mounted a bluff above the ranch they spotted what they took at first to be more mounted Mexicans, dressed in *serapes* and sombreros. These men waved to them, but it soon became apparent that these were the very Apaches they sought, and both sides opened fire.

Having failed to deceive their pursuers, the Apaches split into two groups. The first group drove their stolen stock towards the Cuchillo Negro Mts approximately 10 miles away. The other Apaches dismounted behind a very gentle rise, and opened fire. They continued this fire until Sgt Williams' party threatened to outflank them on their left, whereupon they remounted and retreated to the next slight fold in the terrain, where they again dismounted and opened fire (see diagram opposite). They successfully repeated these delaying tactics until they reached the Cuchillo Negro Mts, where they occupied a ridge from which they eventually drove off their pursuers.

Victorio's evasion strategy

Victorio used an extended variation of the basic traveling formation as a strategic decoy, to cripple his enemies' ability to pursue the Apaches while simultaneously protecting his families and logistic support. He would take the majority of his warriors and launch raids in one part of the country, allowing another group of mainly women and children with a small warrior escort to move from their current camp to a new site many miles from the area being attacked by Victorio. Thus the Apaches preserved the integrity of their own "logistic base," while targeting the logistics of their opponents.

As Sergeant Williams' detachment works around the flank, the Apache rearguard withdraws to the next elevation

Apache rearguard

○ ○ ○ ○ ○ ○ ○

Mexican flank guard

Lt Burnett's force

Sgt Williams' flanking detachment

Sketch plan of Lt Burnett's skirmish against Nana's warriors on August 16, 1881.

In January 1880, when Victorio and his followers returned to New Mexico from Chihuahua, they were faced with the problem of evading the US troops that had been stationed in southern New Mexico to intercept the Apaches should they attempt to return to their strongholds in the US. During November and December 1879, Victorio's warriors had stolen hundreds of horses and cattle in Chihuahua, and in January 1880 he had to get these through to the Mescalero Apache reservation, about 30 miles east of the White Sands, where they could be sold to unscrupulous traders in exchange for rifles and ammunition. Victorio now employed the same strategic-decoy method to draw a US force under Maj Albert P. Morrow, 9th Cavalry, into pursuing his band of warriors north, from the Goodsight Mts up between the Black Range and the Caballo Mts, as far as the Cuchillo Negro Mts and beyond (see Plate C). On January 16, Victorio had a brief parley at Canada Alamosa with one Andrew Kelley, who would report that the chief was leading approximately 60 well-armed and well-mounted warriors. (Kelley had been an interpreter at Victorio's old reservation at Ojo Caliente, and had also acted as an intermediary between Victorio and the US Army in February 1879.) Once Morrow's pursuit was well underway, a second Apache group drove their large and vulnerable looted herd northeastwards through the area just vacated by the Army, to reach their destination safely.

There was another dividend to be gained from this ploy: drawing the available US troops into a long pursuit over very rough terrain wore out

The general area of the Burnett skirmish, with the Cuchillo Negro Mts on the western horizon. Although the terrain appears to be flat, there are very gentle undulations in the plain; these gave the Apaches enough cover to mount a running rearguard action against their pursuers until they reached the cover of the mountains. (Author's photo)

21

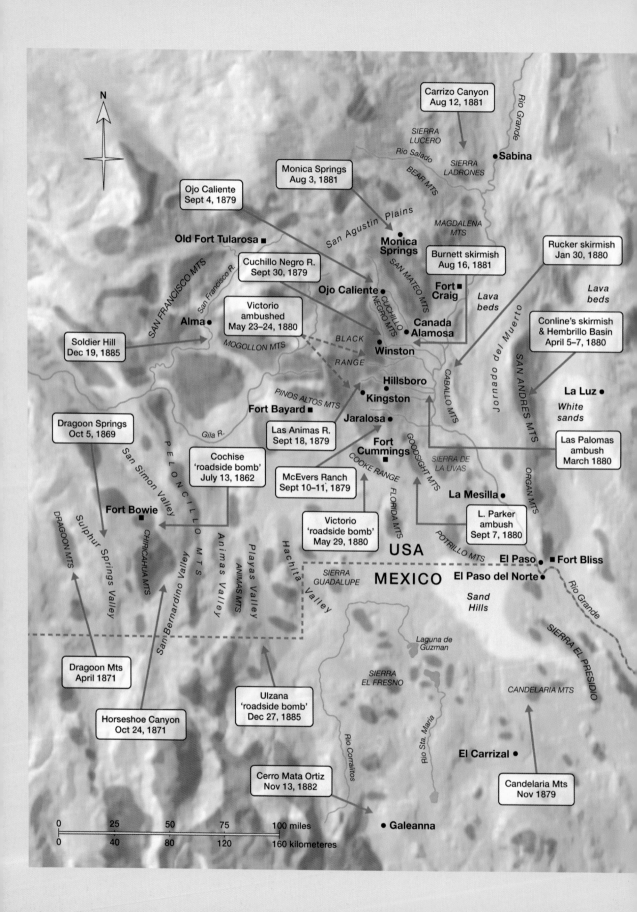

N

Carrizo Canyon
Aug 12, 1881

Rio Grande

SIERRA
LUCERO

Rio Salado

SIERRA
LADRONES

• Sabina

Monica Springs
Aug 3, 1881

San Agustin Plains

MAGDALENA
MTS

Ojo Caliente
Sept 4, 1879

Old Fort Tularosa ■

Monica
Springs

SAN MATEO MTS

Burnett skirmish
Aug 16, 1881

Rucker skirmish
Jan 30, 1880

Cuchillo Negro R.
Sept 30, 1879

Fort
Craig ■

*Lava
beds*

*Lava
beds*

SAN FRANCISCO MTS

San Francisco R.

Ojo Caliente •

CUCHILLO
NEGRO MTS

Conline's skirmish
& Hembrillo Basin
April 5–7, 1880

Victorio
ambushed
May 23–24, 1880

Canada
Alamosa

Alma •

BLACK

RANGE

Winston •

CABALLO MTS

SAN ANDRES MTS

Jornada del Muerto

Soldier Hill
Dec 19, 1885

MOGOLLON MTS

La Luz •

*White
sands*

Hillsboro •

Kingston •

PINOS ALTOS MTS

Fort Bayard ■

Las Palomas
ambush
March 1880

Dragoon Springs
Oct 5, 1869

Gila R.

Las Animas R.
Sept 18, 1879

Jaralosa •

GOODSIGHT MTS

Fort
Cummings ■

SIERRA DE
LA UVAS

La Mesilla •

Cochise
'roadside bomb'
July 13, 1862

McEvers Ranch
Sept 10–11, 1879

COOKE RANGE

ORGAN MTS

San Simon Valley

PELONCILLO MTS

L. Parker
ambush
Sept 7, 1880

Fort Bowie ■

Victorio
'roadside bomb'
May 29, 1880

FLORIDA MTS

USA

POTRILLO MTS

El Paso • ■ Fort Bliss

DRAGOON MTS

Sulphur Springs Valley

CHIRICAHUA MTS

San Bernardino Valley

Animas Valley

ANIMAS MTS

Playas Valley

Hachita Valley

MEXICO

El Paso del Norte •

Rio Grande

Dragoon Mts
April 1871

SIERRA
GUADALUPE

*Sand
Hills*

SIERRA EL PRESIDIO

Horseshoe Canyon
Oct 24, 1871

Ulzana
'roadside bomb'
Dec 27, 1885

*Laguna de
Guzman*

SIERRA
EL FRESNO

CANDELARIA MTS

Rio Corralitos

Rio Sta. Maria

El Carrizal •

Cerro Mata Ortiz
Nov 13, 1882

Candelaria Mts
Nov 1879

0   25   50   75   100 miles

0   40   80   120   160 kilometeres

• Galeanna

the men and mounts of these overstretched units. The Apaches could keep ahead of the soldiers on foot if needs be, but if they were on horseback it was well-nigh impossible to maintain a successful pursuit. During this strategic movement Victorio chose to fight several skirmishes, which Maj Morrow interpreted as rearguard actions to protect Apache dependants – yet Victorio was apparently completely unencumbered with either families or loot. The reason for allowing the 9th Cavalry to get within range to fight these skirmishes was to foster an illusion among the pursuers that, with a little extra effort, victory would be within their grasp. Having achieved both their aims – to decoy the cavalry away from the route of the Apaches' plundered herd, and to tire them out – the warriors broke contact at a time of their own choosing. By the end of this pursuit, the editor of *The Grant County Herald* reported on February 21, 1880 that:

> [Morrow's] men were ragged, many of them barefooted, and nearly one half without horses. All were hungry and jaded. Officers and men had been messing in common, and the sick list was increasing daily. In short the command, which had been kept on the move almost constantly for six weeks, was in no condition to continue the campaign.

The last sentence is of special significance. Major Morrow was highly praised for his and his men's perseverance during several long pursuits of Victorio in 1879 and 1880 – but in fact, these displays of dogged stamina to the point of exhaustion were exactly what the Apache leader wanted to provoke.

THE AMBUSH

The basic aim of the ambush was to cripple the enemy's ability to respond to the first volley. The ambush site would often be chosen so as to allow the Apaches to fade back into rough terrain should this first volley fail to be crippling – if the target either detected the ambush in time, or elected to stand and fight rather than flee. The ambush would ideally be delivered from close

C   THE THEATER OF OPERATIONS, 1879–81

This sketch map of southern New Mexico and northern Chihuahua, with parts of Arizona to the west and West Texas to the east, shows only major terrain features, the US Army posts and settlements mentioned in the text, and the approximate sites of the actions described. The Fort Apache reservation, north of the Salt River, and the San Carlos agency, south of that river, are off the map to the west – Ft Apache was perhaps 80 miles northwest of Old Fort Tularosa. The Mescalero reservation is off the map to the east, about 20 miles northeast of La Luz, in the edge of the Sacramento Mountains. Tres Castillos, where Victorio was killed, is about 20 miles east of the bottom right hand corner of the map. (Other Army posts briefly mentioned in the text are Fort Wingate, which is far to the northwest of the map; and Fort Stanton, which is off the map about 100 miles east of Fort Craig.)

The two US Army regiments that provided the permanent garrisons in New Mexico – the 9th Cavalry and 15th Infantry – were understrength, and usually had to operate in very modest dispersed detachments often of fewer than 30 soldiers. A cavalry regiment had 12 companies (or "troops"), so was divisible into three battalions (or "squadrons"). A company was supposed to have about 80 all ranks, but this was never achieved on the frontier. For example, in October 1879, Maj Albert P. Morrow's battalion of the 9th Cavalry from Fort Bayard consisted on paper of five companies; but Co A had 28 enlisted men, Co B counted 23, Co C had 25, Co G numbered 32, and Co H had only 15 – a total of just 123 NCOs and troopers. On October 23, Maj Morrow also had attachments of the 34-man Co A from 6th Cavalry, and about the same number of Apache scouts; but by the time Victorio and Juh ambushed him on October 27, in the Guzman Mts, after leading him across the parched sandhills of northern Chihuahua, Morrow had just 81 thirsty troopers of the 9th and 6th Cavalry, and 18 of Lt Gatewood's scouts.

range without any warning. The first targets would usually be their enemy's horses, as the minimum aim of the ambush was to hinder the enemy's ability to continue their pursuit.

The Apaches were masters of concealment, being able to hide quickly in apparently barren terrain – even bare grassland – but when they had time they could prepare hidden and protected positions. While the Apaches were, on average, poor marksmen, their first shots were usually quite accurate, since they generally chose positions that allowed them to rest their firearms and take steady aim, at ranges short enough to maximize the effect of the opening volley. (It should also be noted that their opponents were usually not particularly good shots themselves; the US Army could not afford the extra ammunition to provide its troops with regular target practice, and did not begin to discuss a remedy to this situation until 1880. Reports of a number of actions also make clear that the Apaches sometimes enjoyed superior close-range firepower, having Winchester repeaters against the Army's single-shot Springfield "trapdoor" breech-loaders.)

A number of variations in the type of ambush employed by the Apaches in the 1870s and 1880s can be identified. These fall into four broad categories: planned, killing, decoy, and *ad hoc* ambushes – although these were not always clearly distinct (for example, an *ad hoc* ambush might have used decoys in order to lure the enemy into position). The following examples are grouped according to the principal element of the ambush techniques employed on each occasion.

Planned ambushes: Ojo Caliente, September 4, 1879

The Apaches were known to watch their targets for a number of days in order to identify any exploitable weaknesses in their routine. On September 4, 1879, Victorio and a number of warriors attacked the horse herd belonging to Company E, 9th Cavalry, then stationed (under Capt A.E. Hooker, an officer who was both severe and incompetent) at Victorio's favorite camping ground at Ojo Caliente. They killed the five men guarding the 50 horses and 18 mules, and drove off the entire herd without alerting the rest of the garrison. They were able to do this by watching the horse-herders' routine patiently, and only striking when the herd was out of sight and earshot of the rest of the garrison. The Apaches noted that each day the horses and mules were taken out to graze further and further up the valley from the post, and that as the herd turned back towards Ojo Caliente it passed through an area on the far side of a low ridge, which was slashed with a number of *arroyos* (stream-beds) running down to the more level ground. While the herd was driven along the side of the ridge and across these arroyos the guards appear to have been in the habit of stopping for a rest, and it was at this moment that the Apaches struck.

When the ground was examined after the attack, it was noted that the Apaches had divided into three groups. The first, about 12–15 strong, had been tasked with killing the guards, and had concealed themselves around the area where the troopers (who were armed only with revolvers) took their break. There is some indication that this spot was not fixed, as there were signs that these Apaches had quietly fallen back in the face of the advancing herd until the guards stopped. Other dismounted Apaches were concealed along the flanks of the herd's advance, to drive the horses and mules down an arroyo; and a third group were concealed in another arroyo further down the ridge, to head off any animals which tried to return to Ojo Caliente.

Apaches regarded the horse with a good deal less reverence than the Plains Indians. They rarely fought on horseback, and regarded horses simply as a way to move rapidly around the country – and as food, if necessary. A participant in one of the 10th Cavalry's engagements in West Texas recalled seeing Apaches employing classic "mounted infantry" tactics – fighting on foot, mounting to ride to a new position, then dismounting to resume firing. (Courtesy Arizona Historical Society, no. 47493)

Three of the five guards were believed to have been dismounted when the Apaches opened fire, while the two men still mounted were thought to have been shot out of the saddle as the herd stampeded down the arroyo. The tracks showed that at least some of the horses had tried to turn back towards Ojo Caliente before the mounted Apaches had headed them off, collected the herd and driven them away.

By the time the herd was missed at Ojo Caliente the Apaches had a two-hour start over the now practically dismounted garrison (a courier had to be sent for help mounted on the single remaining mule). Company E did not receive remounts until December 1879, thus preventing them from taking part in the Army's pursuit of Victorio in September and October 1879. This pursuit ended when the Apaches slipped into Mexico, and fought off their exhausted pursuers in the mountains near Laguna de Guzman in Chihuahua on the night of October 27/28.

Cuchillo Negro river, September 30, 1879

On September 29, 1879, Apache scouts led by Lts Augustus P. Blocksom and Charles Gatewood, 6th Cavalry, supported by troopers from Maj Morrow's 9th Cavalry command, attacked Victorio's camp near the Cuchillo Negro river. They managed to kill two Apache warriors and one woman before the rest made good their escape into the surrounding mountains as darkness fell. Gatewood and Blocksom pitched their camp about half a mile up the canyon from that set up by Morrow's 9th Cavalry detachment. Early the following morning the Apache scouts fanned out from their camp in search of the hostiles, leaving Gatewood and Blocksom in their camp with a detachment of 6th Cavalry troopers (the latter being attached to Indian Scout companies simply to guard their mule-train). In the meantime, some of Victorio's warriors had infiltrated the heights around Morrow's camp, and others had slipped into positions above the 6th Cavalry detachment.

The hostiles waited until breakfast, when Maj Morrow withdrew 11 out of 12 men from guard duty on the bluffs surrounding his camp. The remaining sentry was shot through the head by an Apache sniper, while the rest of the Apaches opened a hot fire from all sides into both camps. Gatewood recorded the confusion caused by this attack:

> Early next morning, as we had just finished breakfast, a single shot rang out down the canyon, then a volley, suddenly increasing into more shots and more volleys, with sounds of command, all doubled and trebled in reverberations up the valley, until it was one roar of pandemonium that was enough to set a nervous man wild. I didn't believe there was a sane man in the country, except the Corporal, who coolly informed me after a while that I was sitting on the wrong side of a rock, and pointed out to me the folly of protecting a rock.

The deadlock was broken by the storming of one of the bluffs by the 6th Cavalrymen, who then provided covering fire as Maj Morrow led an assault on another bluff. At this point the Apache scouts returned, and Victorio's men pulled back into the mountains. Morrow later reported that he had driven off the Apaches, but had had to withdraw through lack of water; Gatewood told a very different story, however, stating that the hostiles had withdrawn to better positions from which they could not be dislodged. When Morrow started to withdraw these Apaches returned to the attack, and harassed the command

until it reached more open ground. The key point to note is that the hostile Apaches were familiar enough with US Army routine to strike the command when it was at its most vulnerable.

Santa Cruz Mountains, May 15, 1886

This was another occasion when monitoring of their enemy's routine paid handsome dividends for the Apaches. On May 14, 1886, Apache raiders stole 30 horses from a ranch near the Santa Cruz Mts in Sonora, Mexico. The raiders struck in the mid-afternoon, and as darkness approached one of the ranch hands contacted Company D, 4th US Cavalry, commanded by Capt Charles Hatfield. This detachment – consisting of the captain, 37 cavalrymen, and two Mexican guides named Moreno and Mendez – set out in pursuit, following the trail into the mountains until darkness fell. The following day Hatfield's detachment neared the top of the mountains, and discovered the Apache camp. The nature of the terrain meant that much of the pursuit had been conducted by dismounted men leading their horses. Hatfield now assigned double the usual number of mounts to his horse-holders (seven or eight each, instead of the usual four), while the rest of his men charged into the camp. The Apaches scattered, and Hatfield reported capturing 21 horses and camp equipment. The captain quickly realized that getting his command and their recaptured horses out of the mountains would be difficult should the Apaches choose to counterattack.

By throwing out a dismounted skirmish line to the front, and assigning a few men to guard the captures and the troops' own mounts and mules, he managed to get clear of the mountains without further contact with the hostiles. Once back on more or less level terrain, Hatfield reorganized his small command into three groups. A sergeant and 14 dismounted men took the lead in skirmish order. These were preceded by a single mounted man, and flanked by a mounted trooper at each end of the line; this group was also accompanied by Moreno and Mendez. Hatfield himself, with 12 troopers, took charge of the led troop horses; he was followed by seven men driving the mule-train and the captured horses. The detachment had to pass through some more rough terrain before they could reach the relative safety of the town of Santa Cruz. Passing through a narrow canyon, the advance guard found a spring sufficient to supply the needs of both men and animals, the latter having been without water for more than 24 hours.

The reason for the lack of contact during the descent out of the mountains was that the Apaches had moved ahead of the command, watching Hatfield's movements, and had set up positions above and beyond this spring in anticipation that he would have to use it. They let the advance element take water and then move on – doubtless noting that this group had drawn ahead of the two parties with the horses (in spite of explicit orders from Hatfield to his sergeant not to allow such a gap to develop). The Apaches allowed Hatfield to water the troop horses, and only struck when the last group of seven men with the mule-train and captured horses reached the spring.

They opened up a withering fire from the rocks, causing a momentary panic among the troopers when their sergeant was wounded. Both Hatfield's and the final group were then pinned down for half an hour, before some of the advance detachment returned and helped to extricate the trapped men. This involved a further vigorous exchange of fire, during which a trapped and wounded man was shot dead by the Apaches at the very moment of his rescue. The captain then ordered the survivors to withdraw. Hatfield suffered two men killed and two sergeants wounded, and lost his mules (which would have been carrying food and probably extra ammunition), and the Apaches recaptured their horses. The captain also lost his own personal mount, and three troop horses which were forgotten in the heat of the action. There was no indication of any casualties sustained by the Apaches.

Here we can see the rapidity with which Apaches could size up a situation and plan an effective ambush at relatively short notice. It also shows the discipline exercised by the warriors in not opening fire until the optimum moment. Such discipline was crucial to the success of a ruthlessly efficient double ambush executed by Victorio in the Candelaria Mountains of Mexico.

The killing ambush: Candelaria Mountains, November 1879 (see Plate D)

We are lucky to have reports of this incident – which virtually exterminated two parties of Mexican militia from the village of El Carrizal – from Mexicans and Texas Rangers who reached the scene less than two weeks after the event, and later recollections from James Kaywaykla, who as a very young Warm Springs Apache warrior took part in the first phase of the double ambush. Kaywaykla clearly describes how Victorio assigned leadership of different elements of this ambush to various senior members of his following. Both the Apaches and Texas Rangers state that there were no survivors from this first party of 14 militiamen (though a Mexican source implies the survival of one wounded man).

While the first phase was accomplished by skillful positioning and concealment and good fire-discipline, the second not only reinforces the impression of Victorio's control over his warriors, but also suggests his exploitation of a knowledge of his opponents' culture, and of their supposed understanding of Apache tactics. As reconstructed by the Texas Rangers who helped recover the bodies, the Apaches – most unusually – did not immediately withdraw after wiping out the first party of El Carrizal irregulars, but remained at the ambush site over two nights. Victorio apparently anticipated that a second party of Mexicans would come looking for their comrades, and that they would be confident that the Apaches had left the area. (If the Mexican source is correct that a wounded survivor was discovered, that would have reinforced this belief.) The second party gathered up the bodies of their fellow villagers, and dug a grave; and it was only when the men were grouped around the grave that the Apaches opened fire. The author would suggest that this indicates that Victorio knew enough about how Mexicans would react on discovering the bodies to catch them at their most vulnerable. Most of the second party were killed; a number of them managed to break out of the trap and some of these escaped completely, but one was found to have been cut off and killed after getting 600 yards into open country, and two others were never found. A local Mexican source writing within days of the event acknowledged the loss of a total of 33 men in the double ambush.

This ambush underlines the patience and discipline exercised by the Apaches. In all likelihood, most if not all of them were in position during the whole time the second group of Mexicans were gathering up their dead for burial, and not one of these warriors betrayed his presence. In comparison with the "coup-counting" Plains Indian culture of the 1860s–70s, Apache culture did not reward displays of individual boldness, but rather the ability to follow the directions of a respected leader. A young Apache who opened fire prematurely and ruined an ambush would be marked as unreliable, even dangerous, and would be shunned by his peers.

Evidence reported by the Texas Rangers also showed the Apaches' adherence to the principle of minimum exposure to risk. One Mexican had crawled into a crevice from which he could shoot anyone coming at him from either east or west, and was hidden from warriors on the cliffs above him. However, his legs were exposed to Apache riflemen on the opposite (north) side of the canyon, and – instead of rushing him, which would certainly have allowed him to shoot down at least one of them – the latter had aimed at his legs and "literally shot them off up to his knees." The Apaches probably sustained few, if any casualties in either of these ambushes.

Ambushes by decoy

This term needs to be defined with some care. Apaches often used decoy tactics of one sort or another to lull their targets into a false sense of security, and these were usually more subtle than those used by the Plains Indians. A classic Plains Indian ploy was to send out a small party of warriors to draw the enemy into a pursuit of this visible target, which then tried to lead the pursuers into an ambush by a far larger force. The obvious example of this technique is the destruction of Capt William J. Fetterman's command near Fort Phil Kearny on December 21, 1866 by Lakota, Cheyenne and Arapaho warriors.

While Apaches did occasionally employ this type of tactic (e.g. at Cerro Mata Ortiz in November 1882 – see below), their techniques were usually more indirect. In the "Fetterman massacre," the decoys and the intended target were both aware of each other's presence, and the aim was to draw Fetterman's detachment on, by the promise of an easy victory, into a deadly trap. By contrast, the aim of Apache decoys was usually to lull the enemy into a false sense of security just prior to the ambush. The tracks of their horses could be laid in such a manner as to deceive the enemy into thinking that there were no Apaches in the near vicinity. Noise, such as gunfire, could be used to draw the enemy through a prepared ambush. Closer to the classic Plains technique was the encouragement of an enemy to launch an attack by allowing him to sight Apaches who were acting as if they were unaware of his presence, thus encouraging him to follow them into terrain that he would normally have avoided. Likewise, decoys might also simulate sudden panic upon apparently sighting their foes, to provoke a charge that would spring an ambush laid between the decoys and the enemy.

Decoys by tracks: Horseshoe Canyon, October 24, 1871
(see Plate E2)

On October 21, 1871, Apaches attacked a small ranch about 25 miles from Camp (later Fort) Bowie in the San Simon Valley in southern Arizona. Two men, Richard Barnes and R.M. Gilbert, were in one of the two adobe buildings; some of the Apaches quietly occupied the vacant building during the night, and fatally wounded Barnes the following morning when he emerged from the other building. Gilbert, though suffering from fever, temporarily drove the Apaches back into cover with his Henry repeating rifle, and managed to drag his comrade back into the house. The Apaches then placed the building under siege, and managed to wound Gilbert. When they subsequently set the roof on fire, Gilbert, realizing that Barnes was beyond aid, blasted his way free and managed to reach good cover. The Apaches knew where he was, but could not finish him off without great risk from his

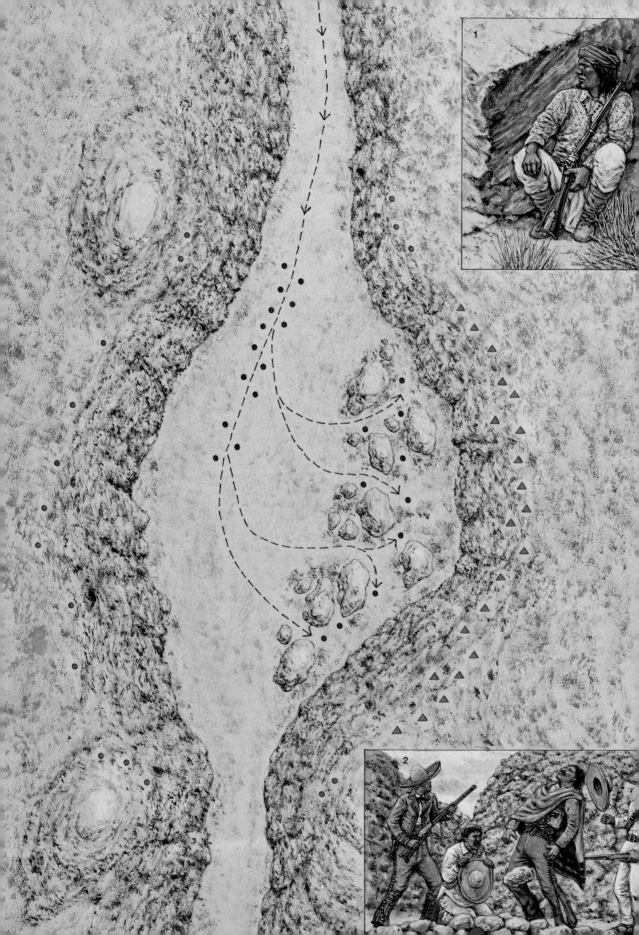

rapid-fire weapon, so they left him to the mercy of the terrain. The following day Gilbert managed to reach help; that night he was brought into Camp Bowie, and the alarm was raised.

Twenty-five men from the 3rd US Cavalry led by Capt Gerald Russell and accompanied by civilian guide Robert H. Whitney set out in pursuit, and trailed the Apaches (possibly led by Juh) into the Chiricahua Mountains. On October 24, approximately 40 miles from Bowie, Russell's detachment was ambushed in Horseshoe Canyon. The Apaches had used a false trail to convince Russell that it was safe to approach the waterhole there; they had left a clear trail both into and then out of the box canyon. After traveling away from the canyon mouth they had turned up into the mountains, and returned to occupy the high ground surrounding Horseshoe Canyon. When Russell arrived in the mid-afternoon he found himself pinned down until nightfall; Whitney and two horses were killed, and a cavalryman was wounded. Russell claimed to have killed many warriors, but withdrew under the cover of darkness and saw no bodies. From the Apache point of view, the light casualties inflicted on their pursuers were irrelevant – they had succeeded in their aim of terminating Russell's pursuit.

A more common technique was for the Apaches to lay a trail that passed through the ambush zone, and then to simply double back on the flanks to take up concealed positions. Captain Russell himself had been caught in just such an ambush in the Dragoon Mts in April 1871, six months before and some 35 miles west of his action in Horseshoe Canyon (see Plate E1). With approximately 30 troops and a guide, he had pursued the trail of a large group of Apaches led by Cochise into the Dragoons. Russell's guide Merejildo Grijalva became convinced that the Apaches were waiting to ambush them if they proceeded any further. As they commenced their withdrawal, they found that Cochise's warriors had circled around behind the troops and occupied both sides of the canyon. Despite the heavy fire opened upon them as they rode out, on that occasion Russell managed to extricate his men from the trap without casualties.

The increased sophistication of the October ambush in Horseshoe Canyon even raises the intriguing possibility that at least some of these Apaches had earlier been involved in the April skirmish in the Dragoon Mountains. The

D **KILLING AMBUSH: CANDELARIA MOUNTAINS, NOVEMBER 7 & 9, 1879**

This reconstructs a successful double-stage ambush planned and sprung by Victorio.

In the first phase, the Chiricahuas were lying in wait, on either side of a canyon, for a party of about 14 Mexican irregulars from the village of El Carrizal. Once the Mexicans (**blue spots**) had ridden into the canyon, warriors whom Victorio had posted each side of the entrance and exit of the killing-ground, and others along the slope to the Mexicans' right (**red spots**), opened fire. The Mexicans' horses were the primary target of this first fusillade. Seeing an apparently obvious source of cover, the Mexicans ran to take shelter among the scatter of large boulders to their left. At that point the majority of the Apaches, who were waiting in concealment along the top of that slope (**red triangles**), opened fire from above and behind them. The Mexicans were wiped out.

In a remarkable example of his hold over his followers, Victorio, judging that a search party would come looking for the first, did not move off at once – the almost invariable Apache practice. Instead, the Chiricahuas remained on the spot for 48 hours, and were under cover (**inset 1**) when, on November 9, a second party of 20–30 riders from El Carrizal and the Samaniego ranch duly arrived – probably feeling secure in the knowledge that Apaches always withdrew immediately after a clash. The Mexicans gathered up the bodies of their relatives and neighbors, and proceeded to dig a mass grave for them. The position of the corpses of men from this second party suggested that the Apaches waited until they were gathered in a compact group around the grave before springing the trap (**inset 2**). Some of the survivors managed to ride out of the canyon and make good their escape, but others were ridden down and killed. The total Mexican losses to this double ambush were reported as 33 men killed.

The left-hand man in this group photo of Apache scouts is the guide Merejildo Grijalva, a Mexican who escaped after being captured by Cochise, and scouted for the US Army for many years. It was he who warned Capt Russell, 3rd Cavalry, of the imminent ambush in the Dragoon Mts in April 1871. While the Apaches carry single-shot Springfield M1873 carbines, Grijalva clearly has a repeating rifle. (Courtesy Arizona Historical Society, no. 43387)

relatively low numbers involved in this guerrilla warfare meant that quite junior leaders in the US Army would have been easily recognized by the Apaches, in whose culture the qualities of an individual were important. It is tempting to imagine that in October some of the Apaches might have recognized Russell, and agreed that since this officer might have learned from the earlier ambush, they should try a different variation this time.

Las Animas river, September 18, 1879

A third example of a decoy ambush by tracks was that sprung upon two companies of the 9th Cavalry in the Black Range around the headwaters of the Rio Las Animas on September 18, 1879. Here an obvious trail up into the mountains led through and beyond the chosen ambush site; the Apaches then took up positions around and above this trail, and waited. About 40 "buffalo soldiers" from Companies A & B, 9th Cavalry, led by Capt Byron Dawson and accompanied by four Navajo scouts, were following the trail.

Despite the Navajos' unease as to the wisdom of following the trail, Dawson pressed on, and in mid-morning the detachment suddenly came under fire from above and all around. One of the Navajos was killed in the opening volley, but most of the Apache fire seems to have been aimed at Dawson's horses. The troopers took cover as best they could, but found themselves pinned down in a murderous crossfire from which they could neither advance nor retreat. By noon, Dawson's men were running low on ammunition; but help then arrived in the form of Companies C & G of the 9th, accompanied by civilian volunteers from the Hillsboro mining camp. However, these reinforcements were soon pinned down in their turn. Although they were only able to pull out as darkness fell, the casualties were again surprisingly low – two Navajo scouts, one civilian, and two, perhaps three 9th Cavalrymen. Their horse casualties were far higher; the regiment's monthly return acknowledged 29 horses killed in action, while the Fort Bayard return stated the loss of 28 horses (but admitted that some of these had escaped rather than been killed). It was acknowledged that the detachment had to abandon much equipment in their withdrawal, and the bodies of those killed were not recovered until almost a week later. There is some suspicion that one or two of these men might have been alive and missed in the darkness when the detachment withdrew. From the Apache point of view, a simple decoy trail into an ambush had crippled the ability of four companies of the 9th Cavalry to maintain their immediate pursuit, and forced them to abandon much equipment to the Apaches.

Near Bavispe, Sierra Madre Mountains, April 24 or 26, 1883

In 1883, Gen George Crook mounted an expedition, spearheaded by a large number of Apache scouts, into the Sierra Madre Mts of northern Mexico in pursuit of hostile Apaches. However, before Crook's expedition surprised the hostiles and negotiated their surrender, they received news of an ambush sprung on local troops. The Apaches had stolen a number of cattle from around the villages of Bavispe and Bacerac and had driven them up into the mountains. Some 50 men of the Sonora *Guardia Nacional* from these villages took up the trail, and as they were making their way up a steep slope they were ambushed. The Apaches had set up small stone breastworks across and to either side of the trail; these had been covered over with dry grass, and were virtually invisible until the Apaches delivered a volley at point-blank range from three sides. Four men were killed and two others severely wounded, and the surviving National Guardsmen fell back. They were joined by Mexican Federal troops who had been following them up, but by the time they returned to the scene of the attack the Apaches were long gone.

Decoy by gunfire: McEvers Ranch, September 10–11, 1879

A week after they had taken the horse herd of Company E, 9th Cavalry at Ojo Caliente (see above), Victorio's warriors attacked a Mexican settlement at Jaralosa, approximately 56 miles south of Ojo Caliente. Here they killed between seven and ten men, women and children. Word of the attack reached the mining settlement of Hillsboro approximately 20 miles to the north, and men saddled up and rode south to render what assistance they could. The pursuit does not appear to have been very well organized; the numbers involved are unclear, and the men did not ride together as a single group.

When the Hillsboro men arrived at Jaralosa they were outraged by what they found there. One William Bates, interviewed in 1940, recalled that the bodies showed evidence of extremely cruel deaths; even today, some descendants of people who lived in the area at the time recall this as an atrocity even by Apache standards.

Almost before this ghastly spectacle had sunk in, the posse heard gunfire from the direction of McEvers Ranch, some 2 miles to the southeast of Jaralosa. The haphazard pursuit was continued in that direction, and the Hillsboro men ran piecemeal into an ambush in which between ten and 18 of them were reported as being killed.

Author's suggested site for the McEvers Ranch ambush of September 10, 1879; the posse's starting point at Jaralosa is off the top of the sketch map, and their destination at the ranch is a few hundred yards off the bottom left. Riders following the road **(double broken lines)** roughly southwards would pass on their left a stretch of marshy *cienega*, and on their right some hills and ridges – only about 50ft high, but steep, and offering many natural firing positions close above the trail at **(B)**, **(C)** and **(D)**. Once the posse reached **(A)** the Apaches could bring them under fire from three directions at close range. Any survivors could have found cover in the marshland, but if the Apaches had placed riflemen at **(E)** they would have been pinned down there. Point **(F)** would have provided an excellent vantage point, from which Victorio or whoever else directed this ambush could signal instructions to his warriors.

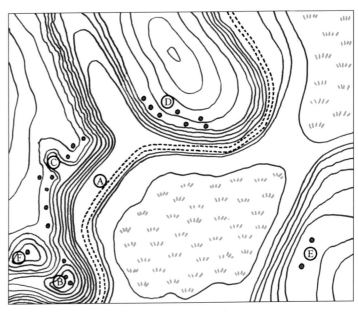

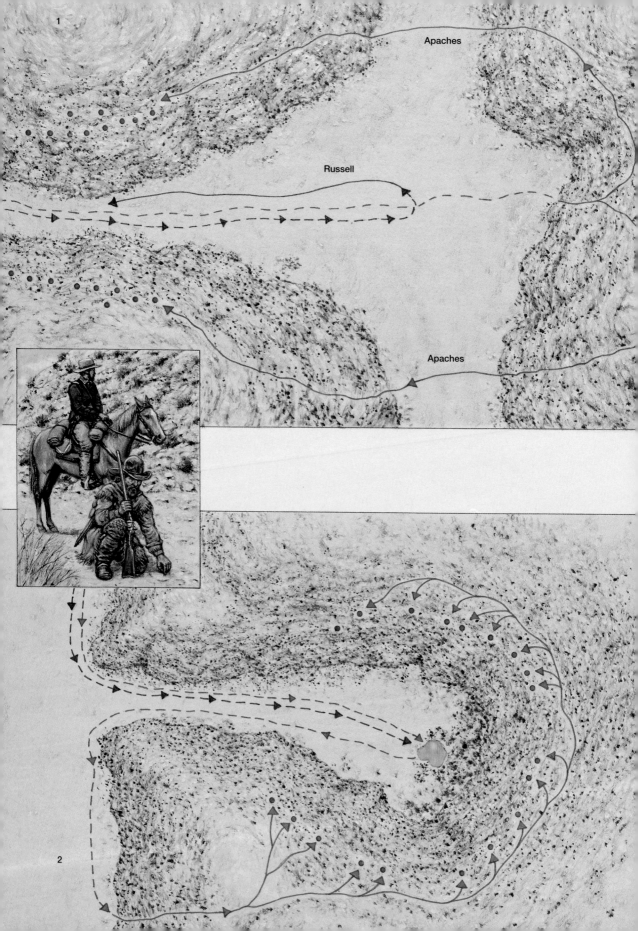

1

Apaches

Russell

Apaches

2

Cave Creek Canyon, looking roughly westwards into the Chiricahua Mountains. This gives a good idea of the difficulty US Army detachments faced in remaining undetected by Apache lookouts, and of the heavy cover on the lower slopes that masked any number of ambush positions. (Photo courtesy Catherine Edwards)

The actual site of the ambush is unknown, but, having examined the terrain, the author believes the most likely spot to be just outside the ranch. The number of fatalities inflicted suggests that the ambush must have been sprung from very close range. There is a ridge further away from the ranch that is said to be the ambush site; however, the terrain there does not offer easy escape routes from positions close to the trail, and if the Apaches had been deployed along the ridgeline itself they would have been too far away to inflict such casualties. The spot where we believe the ambush occurred allows good concealment close to the road, with good escape routes. The killing ground is just beyond a blind corner, and the terrain does not look

E   AMBUSH BY DECOY TRAILS

1: Dragoon Mountains, April 1871

Captain Gerald Russell of the 3rd US Cavalry, with about 30 troopers and a Mexican guide, was following the trail of a large group of Chokonen Chiricahua led by Cochise. As they followed the trail along a canyon in the Dragoon Mts, the scout Merejildo Grijalva became convinced that if they proceeded any further they would run into an ambush. Russell heeded his advice, and the troop began to retrace their steps. The scout had been right: a little further ahead, Cochise had divided his band and sent them doubling back over the high ground to lay an ambush on both sides of the canyon. In fact, he had been hoping to catch Russell from three directions, but the latter's withdrawal after becoming suspicious of the terrain directly ahead of him foiled that part of the plan. Despite heavy fire from both flanks, Russell managed to extricate his men without casualties.

2: Horseshoe Canyon, October 1871

On this occasion Capt Russell was again following the trail of Apache raiders, with 25 troopers and the scout Robert H. Whitney. Seeking to water the horses and men in Horseshoe Canyon in the Chiricahua Mts, Russell and Whitney were deceived by a false trail. The Apaches had also used the waterhole, but had then left clear tracks emerging from the canyon again. Convinced that it was safe, Russell proceeded to the waterhole – unaware that the Apaches had later turned away from their direction of march and up into the high ground, following the upper slopes and dropping off at intervals to lay an almost circular ambush above and around the waterhole. When Russell arrived at mid-afternoon they opened fire, and the troopers were pinned down until Russell managed to lead them out after nightfall. Whitney was killed, as were two horses, and a trooper was wounded; but despite these light casualties, Russell had to give up his pursuit – which had been the Apaches' primary motive.

Inset: Before the enrolment of the Indian Scout companies was promoted by Gen George Crook for his 1872 Tonto Basin campaign, and even afterwards, the experienced advice of local civilian guides, both Mexican and American, was of crucial value. US Army officers new to the Southwest were unfamiliar with the terrain, and anyway lacked any professional grounding in counter-guerrilla tactics. Part of the continued value of white or mixed-blood guides was as interpreters with the Indian Scouts.

An Apache scout poses with what appears to be a Winchester repeater, and a revolver and "butcher knife" at his belt. By the late 1870s many hostile Apaches had also acquired repeating weapons. Lieutenant Charles Gatewood of the Scouts recalled that during the fight against Victorio in the Guzman Mts on October 27, 1879, "The whole top of the mountain was a fringe of fire flashes… the reports from their Winchesters above were so frequent as to be almost a continuous roar." (Courtesy Arizona Historical Society, no. 43391)

particularly threatening until you are well inside the danger area (see sketch map on page 33).

The Apaches' use of decoy techniques is crucial to the understanding of this ambush. A decoy in this sense is any ploy to attract the attention of the target and then draw him into the arranged ambush. In this case the attack upon Jaralosa attracted the attention of the armed civilians at Hillsboro, and what they found when they arrived there enraged them (as the Apaches no doubt intended). Angry men bent on revenge do not think as clearly as they should, and once they had been drawn into the general area, the firing from McEvers Ranch then drew the posse incautiously down the road and into the ambush that had been prepared to receive them. Here the Apaches did not simply monitor the targets' movements and then arrange an ambush in their path; they thought out the sequence of events in advance, and arranged them to manipulate their quarry's reactions. Having sited the ambush in the most advantageous terrain along the posse's predicted line of travel, they fired the decoy shots. These gave the Hillsboro men the impression that another group of settlers might still be rescued from the horrors they had found at Jaralosa, and also that their own approach was undetected – past experience would have suggested that the Apaches tended to flee in the face of substantial and aggressive armed parties. The local newspapers were periodically full of stories about the "cowardly" manner in which Apaches fought; at McEvers Ranch the Apaches apparently took advantage of this reputation and turned it back upon their enemies.

Decoy by simulated innocence: Whetstone Mountains, May 5, 1871

Another form of decoy was to send out one or two men – or, in at least one instance, women – into the open where they knew the enemy would see them. Acting as if unaware of the presence of danger, the decoys would saunter casually into and beyond the killing ground, hoping that they would be followed. Even experienced Indian-fighters could be taken in by this ploy. On May 5, 1871, Lt Howard B. Cushing's detachment was hunting for Cochise when they found a fresh trail left by an Apache woman meandering up a canyon. Though suspicious, they still entered the trap; when they came under fire from Apaches led by Juh, most of the detachment managed to extricate themselves, but Cushing was killed. Sergeant John Mott recorded the quiet discipline of the Apache warriors who attacked them:

The Indians were well handled by their chief, a thick, heavy-set man, who never dismounted from a small brown horse during the fight. They were not noisy or boisterous as Indians generally are, but paid great attention to their chief, whose designs I could guess as he delivered his instructions by gestures.

Decoy by simulated panic: Caballo Mountains, January 30, 1880

Women were also to play a key role in the ambush of Capt Louis B. Rucker in the Caballo Mts during Maj Morrow's pursuit of Victorio in January 1880. Captain Rucker, leading a detachment drawn from Companies B & M, 9th Cavalry, accompanied by civilian volunteers, crossed the Rio Grande following a trail into a canyon (probably Mescal Canyon) at the northern end of the Caballo Mountains. About a mile up the canyon they came upon a herd of livestock guarded by three or four Apache women, who immediately "panicked" and tried to drive the herd up the canyon, thus encouraging Rucker's men into a rash pursuit. As they charged towards the herd they were caught in a crossfire from Apache warriors above and all around them. One Navajo scout was killed and three cavalrymen were wounded. Some of the detachment themselves panicked, and fled all the way back to the other side of the Rio Grande. Rucker, with another officer and ten men, fought a rearguard action back down the canyon, with the Apaches harassing them from the high ground throughout their retreat to the river.

The reporting of this skirmish in the monthly regimental return and the bi-monthly company muster roll is interesting. In the former it is acknowledged that Rucker lost five horses killed in this ambush. The latter claimed that four horses were shot by order due to their exhaustion prior to the ambush, and admitted to only one horse lost. Both sets of records note that three troopers were wounded in action, but give no further detail. However, *The Grant County Herald* reported the details of this skirmish on February 21, 1880. This publication was not particularly well disposed towards the African-American 9th Cavalry, but a private letter from one of Morrow's lieutenants also confirmed that a small detachment had been defeated in the Caballo Mts on January 30.

Mescal Canyon, at the northern end of the Caballo Mts; this is a likely spot for the ambush of Capt Rucker's detachment of the 9th Cavalry on January 30, 1880. This photo was taken about a mile up the canyon from the bank of the Rio Grande; the canyon opens up into a natural amphitheatre before narrowing again, making it an ideal place to station the decoy herd. (Author's photo)

Some of the natural cover along Mescal Canyon, above the natural arena where Capt Rucker is believed to have been ambushed – with such success that some of his troopers fled all the way back and over the Rio Grande. (Author's photo)

An ambush on flat, apparently featureless ground could be even more shocking than a trap laid in a canyon. This is a temporary *arroyo* in Cooke's Canyon, caused by the heavy rains of late July and August; it is close to the trail, and deep enough to shelter a standing man. This gulley is almost invisible from a few yards away, and Apaches often employed such ground for point-blank ambushes on unwary travelers. Five men were killed in this immediate vicinity on May 29, 1880 by Victorio's warriors, who were on their way to Mexico via the Florida Mts, visible on the horizon to the left. (Author's photo)

Ad hoc ambushes: the Apache "roadside bomb"

The rapidly arranged *ad hoc* ambush would be sprung either upon the unexpected appearance of a tempting target, or in an attempt to slow down or cripple a pursuing enemy. One of the things that quickly becomes apparent when traveling in Apacheria is the Apaches' selection of potential ambush sites to catch their enemies off guard. They knew that when passing through a canyon their targets would almost certainly be on the alert for trouble. But by selecting positions in apparently flat terrain, the Apaches could catch their targets off guard, either just before the soldiers increased their state of alertness on entering difficult terrain, or as they breathed a sigh of relief after negotiating it safely. What we might term the Apache "roadside bomb" technique – by analogy with today's IEDs in Iraq and Afghanistan – is typical of the use of apparently innocuous terrain for ambushes.

One ambush of this type was sprung in the aftermath of a major defeat inflicted upon Victorio by Apache scouts on May 24, 1880, in the Black Range in the vicinity of the Palomas river. Several groups of Apaches fled southwards to Mexico, and on May 29 one of these groups spotted a party of five men with a wagon moving towards Cooke's Canyon. Before the entrance to the canyon itself the Apaches occupied a small, narrow arroyo, washed out by the heavy rainfall that periodically strikes the region. These narrow gulleys may be deep enough to conceal a standing man, and are virtually invisible until one stumbles upon them. Where these arroyos converge with or run parallel

The grave of the victims of Ulzana's ambush in the foothills of the Chiricahua Mts on December 27, 1885; the rough inscription reads "Killed by Indians William Reese and Casper Albert Dec 1885." Monuments to soldiers were also sometimes raised, perhaps partly as a warning to recruits; one that can still be seen at Fort Cummings reads: "Sacred to the Memory of Thos Ronan aged 45 LS Hunter aged 33 Chas Devlin aged 28 Thos Daly aged 28 late Privates of Co G 1st Veteran Infantry Cal. Vols. Killed by Apaches at Oak Grove NM Jan 17 1866." (Author's photos)

to the trail, they provide excellent positions from which to open fire at point-blank range without warning. On this occasion the burned wagon and corpses were later found by US troops from Fort Cummings.

Victorio was not the only Apache war chief to use this technique. In November and December 1885 the leader known as Ulzana (Jolsanny/ Josanie) led a small group of warriors up from Mexico to cause havoc in southern New Mexico and Arizona. During the raid he used the "roadside bomb" technique twice: at Soldier Hill on December 19, 1885, and in the Chiricahua Mts on December 27. At Soldier Hill (so-named after the attack), Ulzana's warriors ambushed a detachment from the 8th US Cavalry, killing Surgeon Maddox and four soldiers. The ambush was sprung as the cavalrymen followed a road that curved steadily up a ridgeline towards its summit. The Apaches waited until the detachment had almost reached the top before opening fire, from positions along the crest above and flanking them.

Eight days later, the same Apaches killed two men, William Reese and Caspar Albert, in the eastern foothills of the Chiricahua Mts as they drove a wagon towards Galeyville. There are two possible reconstructions of this ambush. The first is that the wagoners were caught in a close-range crossfire in the riverbed at the bottom of a slope; the other is that they were caught as they rounded a bend and descended towards the ford, by warriors in positions immediately beyond the outer curve of the road. In the latter case, one of the two men would have been wholly occupied with controlling the vehicle, and thus unable to return fire.

This type of ambush was also employed by Apaches in the 1860s when they were more reliant upon bows and muzzle-loading firearms. Cochise used this technique to devastating effect in 1862 near Apache Pass in the Chiricahua Mts, and again at Dragoon Springs in 1869. On July 13, 1862, nine miners traveling west towards Apache Pass were ambushed from close range by a large group of Apaches concealed in a small gulley running parallel to the trail. When the bodies were discovered by US troops it appeared

Naches, of the Central Chiricahua, photographed in middle age; he holds a repeating rifle, apparently a Winchester. While the Apaches did acquire significant numbers of these, usually by trade south of the border, some primary sources and modern battlefield archaeology confirm that in the late 1870s and early 1880s many appreciated the longer effective range of the Springfield "trapdoor" or Remington "rolling block" rifles. (Courtesy Arizona Historical Society, no. 20803)

that all nine men were taken completely unawares by the opening volley, presumably assuming that they were safe on flat, open ground. All were hit, and those not killed outright were quickly finished off, though one man was reported to have been taken alive and burned to death.

At Dragoon Springs, Cochise not only took advantage of the terrain but also used the time of day to lull his target into a false sense of security. As the sun set on October 5, 1869, a coach with six men – the driver, four soldiers from the 21st Infantry, and mine owner John F. Stone – was driving towards Dragoon Springs in the Sulphur Springs Valley. The ground was deceptively flat, and since twilight was drawing in the coach party assumed that they were safe (as mentioned, Apaches did not usually attack at night). Once again, Cochise used a small arroyo close to the road to conceal most of his men. These warriors opened fire as the coach drove past them, killing the driver and three soldiers; Stone and the surviving soldier were cut off and killed by mounted Apaches when the coach team bolted off the road.

Las Palomas, March 1880

The principle of striking immediately before or beyond an obvious ambush point can also be identified in the opportunist ambush of two wagons south of Las Palomas during March 1880, carried out by a small band of Apaches believed to have been led by Nana. (It should be noted that this particular attack has been inflated into a story of the destruction of a whole wagontrain. However, a letter written within a week of the event by an Army doctor who accompanied the Apache scouts who discovered the remains clearly states that only two wagons were involved, and that the Apaches killed five Mexicans and took two children prisoner.)

Once again, their victims were simply in the wrong place at the wrong time. During March 1880 several Apache raiding parties struck the Rio Grande valley in New Mexico. One of these groups of raiders must have spotted these two wagons, and also noted an ideal ambush position along the wagon road where the trail climbed up out of a large, deep arroyo. The two wagons had negotiated the difficult terrain of the riverbed and the steep slope out of it, and had entered what they must have thought was a less dangerous stretch of some 200–300 yards of level road. This illusion was only dispelled when the Apaches opened fire; small hillocks, a ridge only some 20ft high, and a small depression alongside the road offer hiding places within point-blank range in four directions. Lieutenant Thomas Cruse, 6th Cavalry, who commanded the Apache scout detachment that discovered the remains shortly afterwards, wrote in his memoirs that the memory of the sight haunted his sleep for many years.

Goodsight Mountains, September 7, 1880

The more usual *ad hoc* ambush was employed when Apaches were trying to stop or at least slow down an enemy who was in close and vigorous pursuit.

Somewhat confusingly, two officers with the same surname figure in two of the best examples of this type of action.

On September 6, 1880, a stagecoach was ambushed by Apaches in the Goodsight Mts, about 18 miles east of Fort Cummings. When word reached the fort, Col George P. Buell (CO of the 15th US Infantry, and now in field command of operations against the Apaches in southern New Mexico), sent Capt Leopold Parker with Company A, 4th Cavalry, accompanied by ten Apache scouts, towards the scene of the attack, with orders to pick up the trail. Since it was most likely that the raiders would flee into Mexico via either the Florida or the Potrillo Mts, a second company of the 4th was sent directly south to the Floridas to intercept the Apaches should they go that way;

While this is obviously a stiffly posed studio photo, Apaches were known to use the bow and arrows into the 1880s, when it was still an essential weapon for silent hunting. Archaeological evidence strongly suggests that arrows were employed as part of the attempt to stampede Lt Conline's troop horses during his skirmish of April 5, 1880 – see Plate G. (Courtesy Arizona Historical Society, no. 3236)

41

An anonymous grave in Cooke's Canyon; these may be encountered randomly throughout Apacheria, though they are not usually as well preserved as this example. Lieutenant Thomas Cruse, 6th Cavalry, recalled that in 1880 Cooke's Canyon was littered with graves and debris from Apache attacks dating back to the early 1860s. (Author's photo)

if no sign of them was found, this second detachment was to march east to the Potrillo Mountains.

Captain Parker found that the trail of the Apaches ran south along the east side of the Goodsight Mts, and took up the chase; unfortunately, he only assigned two of his men to flanking duty. Towards the southern end of the range he was ambushed by at least 30 Apaches who had concealed themselves along a low ridge; where there was no natural cover, they had constructed small rock breastworks. In the opening volley two Apache scouts and one cavalryman were killed and three more troopers were wounded (including a soldier named Aker, who according to the bi-monthly company muster roll was shot "through fleshy part of thigh and scrotum"). Parker fell back, dismounted, and attempted to drive the Apaches off the ridgeline by advancing in skirmish line with horse-holders to the rear. After several failed attacks he retreated for several miles, and sent to Fort Cummings for support.

Colonel Buell left the fort with a large detachment of the 9th Cavalry under the command of LtCol Nathan Dudley, accompanied by a Gatling gun and a Hotchkiss mountain howitzer. By the time this force arrived, the Apaches were, of course, long gone, having scattered and re-formed some 20 miles further south in the Potrillo Mountains. All Buell saw during the pursuit was a distant dustcloud making its way into Mexico, and when he reached the Potrillos he found that after using the waterhole at their camp site the Apaches had poisoned it with horse entrails. Buell concluded that without a mule-train to carry food and barrels of water, further pursuit was futile. The second 4th Cavalry company, finding no sign of Apaches in the Florida Mts, did not reach the Potrillos until the following day.

In essence, Buell's plan had been perfectly sensible: he correctly predicted the broad movements of the Apaches, and put a plan in place to cut them off. The problem was simply that the speed with which the Apaches could move across country when pursued by a larger force made it almost impossible for US Cavalry to catch up with them without killing or crippling their more

F **ATTACK: CONLINE'S SKIRMISH, APRIL 5, 1880 (I)**

Lieutenant John Conline, with two scouts and 29 troopers of his Co A, 9th Cavalry, was following a trail roughly westwards up Hembrillo Canyon in the San Andres Mountains. Reaching a narrowing of the canyon at about 4.30pm, he halted and sent out videttes – (**2 & 3**) forward to reconnoitre for a possible ambush, and (**1**) to the left and up-slope, to watch that flank and the rear. At some point Conline formed a skirmish line (**4**), with the horse-lines behind and below him (**5**). At c.5.30pm Apaches were spotted moving down the left slope, and then anything up

to 50 more coming fast down the canyon (**6**). The videttes skirmished with the Apaches on the move as they fell back on Conline's main force (**7, and inset**). A warrior identified by the scout José Carillo as Victorio was seen directing his men from high on the northern slope (**8**). A few warriors took up position on the northern slopes (**9**), above and to the right front of Conline. Many more of them used the cover of an *arroyo* cutting up the southern slope of the canyon, which was hidden from the soldiers, to form a firing line (**10–11**). From positions above, to the left of, and facing the troopers, the Apaches engaged them in a fire-fight at a range of some 200 yards.

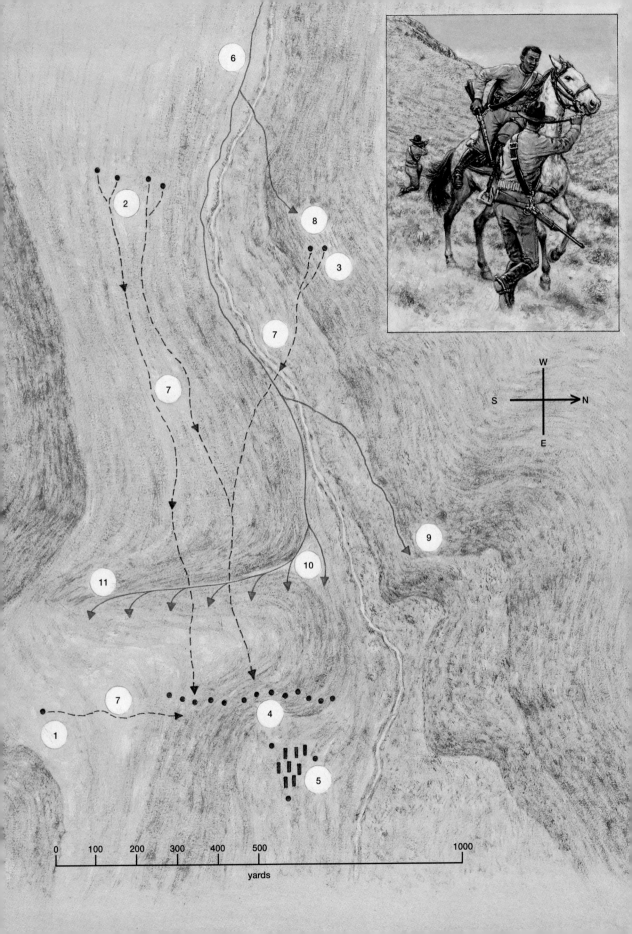

heavily-laden horses in the process. (And even if Buell's plan had worked, the Apaches would simply have scattered once again.) From the Apache viewpoint, they had stopped and fought off the immediate pursuit, allowing them time to put enough distance between themselves and further pursuers to escape into Mexico.

Carrizo Canyon, August 12, 1881

In this case the *ad hoc* delaying ambush evolved into an attack. Nana had come up from Mexico in July 1881, and had commenced raiding far and wide across southern New Mexico. From Fort Wingate, Capt Charles Parker was leading 19 men from Company K, 9th Cavalry and a Mexican scout, as one of a number of detachments of the 9th sent out from Forts Stanton, Cummings, Bayard, Craig and Wingate in an attempt to find the Apaches. On August 11, Parker received a report that Nana had attacked a party of civilians 28 miles to his south and approximately 40 miles from Sabinal, between the Sierra Lucero and the Rio Grande. He reached the spot where the attack had taken place, and followed the Apaches' trail eastwards towards Sabinal.

Despite being covered by a small advance group and flankers, the detachment walked straight into an ambush by well-concealed warriors. Parker later reported that the Apaches had killed the NCO commanding his advance group and flankers with their opening volley. He withdrew some yards and attempted to make a stand, but the Apaches, seeing the damage they had inflicted, chose to press home their advantage and launched an infiltrating attack towards and around his position. Despite losing two killed, and three troopers and the Mexican guide seriously wounded, the detachment held its nerve and shot it out, and the Apaches eventually withdrew. Once again, the important fact for the Apaches was that Parker also lost ten horses shot dead, and had to withdraw to Sabinal; in one sudden ambush Nana had knocked out one of the 9th Cavalry detachments pursuing him. It would be four days before another of these detachments caught up with him (see page 21, for skirmish between Nana's band and Lt Burnett).

THE ATTACK

If Apaches launched a direct attack upon their opponents, it was usually in the aftermath of a particularly successful ambush, when the targets were so demoralized that the Apaches were confident enough to gamble on moving in for the kill. Some Apaches would infiltrate directly towards the enemy, making the maximum use of terrain and cover, while others worked their way around the flanks. Once the use of repeating rifles became common, such attacks could be accompanied by a high rate of fire on the move. This was not usually particularly accurate, but was primarily intended to give an exaggerated impression of the Apaches' strength. These attacks were launched in such a way that if the enemy rallied stubbornly, the Apaches could fade back into cover and disperse with minimal loss – as in the example of Nana's ambush in Carrizo Canyon, cited above.

Cerro Mata Ortiz, November 13, 1882

This was an action between Apaches directed by Juh, Geronimo and Nana, and a small party of Chihuahua state troops led by Juan Mata Ortiz. In November 1882 those Apaches living in the Sierra Madre Mts of Mexico decided to attack the garrison of the small town of Galeana. A later account by Jason Betzinez, who was present, estimated that at this time those Apaches who had left the San Carlos reservation between 1877 and 1882 numbered 75 "first line warriors," plus a large number of youths and older men who would also participate in hostilities if necessary. (It is worth repeating that most of the key leaders present were in fact numbered among these older men.)

Cerro Mata Ortiz, named for the Mexican officer killed with 20 of his Chihuahua state troops when they were ambushed and then surrounded on this low hilltop near the town of Galeana on November 13, 1882. (Author's photo)

Two warriors volunteered to steal horses from the vicinity of Galeana, with the aim of leading any pursuers into an ambush (as noted, the Apaches were willing, where appropriate, to employ such unsubtle Plains Indian-style decoy tactics). Small groups of warriors were hidden in a ravine running alongside the road out of Galeana towards the mountains, and further from the town a large group blockaded the road, hidden by a dip in the terrain. The horses were duly stolen and, as hoped, the thieves were pursued, by a detachment of 22 mounted soldiers (such Mexican state troops, recruited for the short term, were often well armed with Remington carbines and pistols, but suffered from lack of numbers and rudimentary logistics). The decoys stayed out of range, but close enough to draw the pursuers into the trap. The warriors hidden in the roadside ravine let the Mexicans pass, and only opened fire when the latter found themselves confronted by the blocking force.

Fired upon from front and rear, their leader Mata Ortiz made for a nearby low hill or *cerro* (which was later named after him), where his men dismounted and hurriedly raised rock breastworks. The Apaches surrounded the hill, and the older men and some of the better marksmen among them settled in to keep the Mexicans pinned down by fire. All but eight of the remaining warriors started crawling slowly up one side of the hill, while eight younger men, who habitually worked as a team, circled to the opposite side of the hill and did the same. Both groups pushed rocks slightly larger than their heads in front of them to protect themselves from the Mexicans' return fire. Occasionally one of the crawling warriors would pause in his slow progress to fire at the Mexicans. Eventually, the Apaches got to within yards of the surrounded soldiers, whose firing began to dwindle. The Apaches thought that the Mexicans might have run short of ammunition, but suspected that they might receive a volley if they rose to charge. At this point one of the Mexicans managed to mortally wound the cousin of one of the Apaches leading the attack.

This provoked the final assault by the furious Apache leader. It seems that the soldiers were indeed low on ammunition, since the warrior rush was not met with a volley. The Apaches killed all but one of the 22 Mexicans, including Mata Ortiz. One man managed to break out and make a run for Galeana, and Geronimo shouted to let the fugitive go – he might bring out more troops to be ambushed… The Apaches lost only two warriors killed in this fight. Those who had followed Victorio until his death in October 1880 were particularly pleased with the killing of Juan Mata Ortiz, as he had been second-in-command of the Mexican force that finally cornered Victorio at Tres Castillos.

Conline's skirmish, April 5, 1880 (see Plates F & G)

As already stated, it was very rare for Apaches to launch a direct attack upon opponents unless they caught them unawares, and usually such an attack would only be attempted if the odds were stacked in their favor. One example was an action fought on April 5, 1880, when Lt John Conline of Company A, 9th Cavalry, entered Hembrillo Canyon in the San Andres Mts; there he was attacked by a superior force of Apaches, and was probably saved from significant losses, or even disaster, only by the onset of nightfall.

Conline was attached to a battalion of four companies (A, D, F & G) of the 9th Cavalry commanded by Capt Henry Carroll. This was part of a three-battalion force tasked with trying to trap Victorio, who was then believed to be based in the San Andres Mountains. On April 5, Capt Carroll had ordered Conline, with 29 soldiers and two guides, to scout ahead towards the eastern side of the San Andres. During that afternoon they encountered

The view up Hembrillo Canyon from the position of Lt Conline's original skirmish line on April 5, 1880 – see Plate F. Up to 50 Apaches attacked down the canyon towards the camera. Some moved up the slopes on the left of the 9th Cavalry detachment; others infiltrated forwards under cover of the deceptively rough terrain, and a third party worked around Conline's right flank along an *arroyo*, hidden by the green vegetation running from the center to the right of the photograph. (Author's photo)

a trail made by about 50 horses and 100 cattle that led into Hembrillo Canyon. Conline followed these tracks roughly westwards until about 4.30pm. The canyon was starting to narrow, and, concerned about the possibility of an ambush, Conline halted and sent out six men to scout further ahead. At about 5.30pm, Conline spotted two Apaches moving down the slope of the left (south) side of the canyon – and then saw between 35 and 50 more, moving rapidly down the canyon towards him. His advance videttes carried out a fighting withdrawal until they

G **ATTACK: CONLINE'S SKIRMISH, APRIL 5, 1880 (II)**

The initial skirmish line of Conline's detachment (1) was particularly vulnerable on its right flank. While the troopers engaged warriors to their front (2) and above them to the left (3), the Apaches then launched an attack on their right flank (4), working their way forwards over the rough ground on the lower slopes of the canyon's left (southern) side. Some of Victorio's warriors also got into another dry streambed (5–6), which led them all the way around the flank to Conline's right rear (7). From here they opened fire on his horse-lines; at least one Apache climbed the north side of the canyon to fire down (8), and another got into position directly behind the original skirmish line (9). It seems that some troopers from that line, and some of those guarding the horses, then formed a second skirmish line (10) to face this new threat. At about 7.30pm, the determined horseshoe-shaped defense and failing light seem

to have persuaded the Apaches to withdraw up the canyon rather than risk pressing the attack home.

Inset: A warrior creeping up from the dry *arroyo* towards the rear of Lt Conline's right flank; the Apaches were renowned for their skill at concealment in the most rudimentary cover. If they had time to prepare for battle they often stripped to breechclout and moccasins, but would retain items that imparted "war medecine," such as feathered war caps. This Chiricahua, who has followed Victorio from the Warm Springs reservation, also has a beaded "ration ticket" pouch fringed with tin cones. He is armed with an 1873 Winchester carbine; tucked under his cartridge belt is a skull-crushing "floppy-head" warclub for close combat, and he would also certainly be carrying a knife. Despite their fearsome reputation, the Apaches were not generally renowned for marksmanship; on April 5, Lt Conline's company suffered only two men wounded, one horse killed and a second wounded.

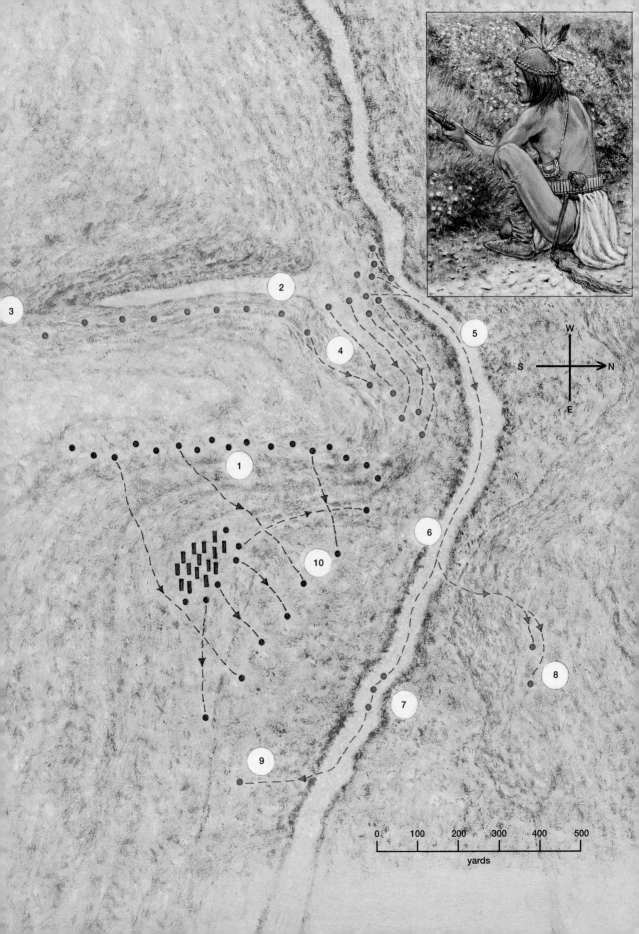

The dry *arroyo* in Hembrillo Canyon used by the Apaches to outflank Conline's troopers on the right. The right-hand end of his original skirmish line was just off the left side of this photograph – see Plate G. (Author's photo)

reached his command. According to Conline, he blocked the Canyon with a skirmish line, and managed to defeat an attempt to turn his flank. The Apaches broke off the engagement at about 7.30pm, allowing the detachment to withdraw with only two men slightly wounded.

The report left by Conline is vivid in its detail; one of his guides, José Carillo, knew Victorio personally, and identified the Apache leader as directing this attack – which, according to Conline, was pressed home with some vigor. This attack was probably born of an attempt to ambush Conline, but the ambush was not sprung because the troopers did not go far enough up the canyon. However, on seeing the size of the detachment and where they had chosen to halt, Victorio must have judged that terrain and numbers were in his favor, and moved down the canyon.

Actual examination of the site revealed that Conline's account was not quite as detailed as it might have been. Conline chose to halt in a less than ideal position, where the Apaches were able to dominate his left flank from above, and to infiltrate to close range through the rough ground immediately to his front. What was worse – and absent from Conline's report – was the fact that they were able to use a dry streambed to turn Conline's right flank, as he did not extend his skirmish line across the whole canyon. Two things probably saved Conline and his men. First, they did not panic, and formed a horseshoe-shaped defense; this faced the Apaches with the prospect of having to move in closer, at the cost of taking too many casualties themselves. Secondly, the approach of nightfall probably convinced the Apaches that the risks were too great and, being reluctant to fight at night, they used the darkness to withdraw.

A direct attack such as that made on Conline was a rarity, but it does show what Apaches were capable of doing if they had superior numbers, modern weapons with plentiful ammunition, favorable terrain, and excellent leadership. The lieutenant and his men were lucky that they had not encountered Victorio earlier in the day. Their calm defense served them well; had they attempted to make a run for it they would have encouraged the Apaches to press home their advantage, and would probably have suffered considerably heavier losses. But neither was the decision to stand fast without its risks: they were hemmed in, and without water other than what remained in their canteens. The calm defense dissuaded the Apaches from moving any closer for fear of taking unacceptable casualties, but Conline's men were exposed to fire from warriors who had infiltrated all round them and who occupied far better protected positions. Had this been earlier in the day, the Apaches would have had the time to sit secure and punish the troopers from safety. Once the Apaches had turned the right flank they were within arrow-range of Company A's horses; at the very least, Conline's horse casualties would have been far more dramatic had this Apache encirclement been achieved earlier in the day.

A cartridge case from a .45/70 Springfield rifle found on the Hembrillo Basin battlefield. The last time it was handled was by one of Victorio's warriors as he closed in on Carroll's troopers early on the morning of April 7, 1880. (Author's photo)

Hembrillo Basin, April 6/7, 1880 (see Plate H)

The Apaches could also combine ambush, attack, and evasion techniques, depending upon the way that events unfolded. Victorio's mixed band of Warm Springs Chiricahua and Mescalero warriors would demonstrate this full range of Apache tactics in the two days following Lt Conline's skirmish.

Late on the evening of April 5, Conline rejoined Capt Carroll's battalion. The latter decided that simply to enter Hembrillo Canyon by the same route was too predictable. He remained unsure as to the location of Victorio's base, but he had to act immediately, since the Apaches might have decided to scatter as a precaution. The following day he sent Lt Patrick Cusack with Companies A & G of the 9th Cavalry back in the direction taken by Conline the previous day. Carroll himself, with the 71 men of Companies D & F, entered the San Andres Mts to the north of Hembrillo Canyon; they followed a roughly parallel canyon, that eventually led them into what is now known as Hembrillo Basin – a wide area high in the San Andres, where Victorio was in fact camped.

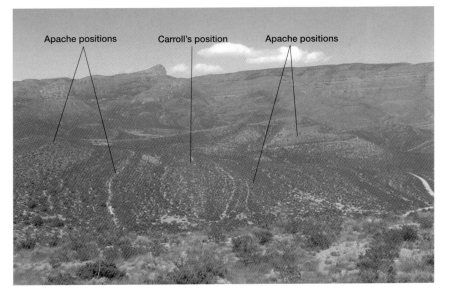

Apache positions   Carroll's position   Apache positions

View of the Hembrillo Basin battlefield looking north from Victorio Ridge, showing the overnight position of Capt Henry Carroll's two companies of the 9th Cavalry on April 6/7 – see Plate H. The lower Apache position on the right represents the infiltrating attacks early on the morning of April 7. Victorio Ridge formed the main position from which Victorio's warriors fought their rearguard action during that day, when US Army reinforcements arrived to relieve Carroll. His command had probably entered Hembrillo Basin somewhere on the center-left horizon. (Author's photo)

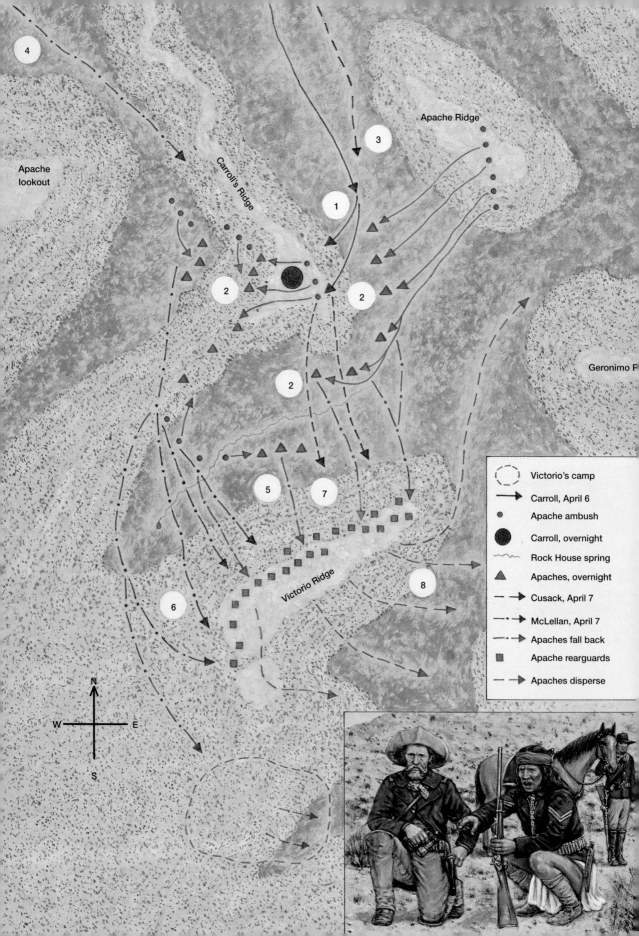

4

Apache
lookout

Apache Ridge

3

Carroll's Ridge

1

2

2

2

Geronimo P

5

7

8

6

Victorio Ridge

N

W — E

S

Victorio's camp

Carroll, April 6

Apache ambush

Carroll, overnight

Rock House spring

Apaches, overnight

Cusack, April 7

McLellan, April 7

Apaches fall back

Apache rearguards

Apaches disperse

Carroll's approach from the north, by a less than obvious route, seems to have taken the Apaches by surprise. Nevertheless, they had time to set up an *ad hoc* ambush designed to stall his advance, and this worked better than expected. Carroll's command found themselves trapped overnight on a low ridge dominated by higher ground, from which the Apaches harassed them thoughout the hours of darkness. The Apaches also stationed men between the soldiers and a small stream that ran below their position, and during the night a number of troopers were wounded during attempts to reach the water.

Apache breastwork in Hembrillo Basin, about 2 feet high and offering good protection for a kneeling rifleman. The viewpoint is roughly from west to east; Carroll's command was pinned down off-camera to the left, and the darker line at top right marks Victorio Ridge, where the warriors held off the US Army reinforcements until their dependants had escaped from the camp site further south. (Author's photo)

In the early morning of April 7, the Apaches started to close in on Capt Carroll's men, and their calculation of the odds encouraged them to attempt infiltrating attacks.

It was only the fortuitous and simultaneous arrival of both Capt McLellan, with two companies of Apache scouts and a company of the 6th Cavalry from another battalion, and of Lt Cusack with the balance of Carroll's battalion, which saved the day. Even so, the Apaches made a steady fighting withdrawal, buying time for their dependants to escape from Hembrillo Basin before they finally dispersed into the mountains. Captain Carroll and seven of his men were seriously wounded (three of the latter later died from their wounds), and it was reported that the Apaches also killed 25 horses and mules and captured four others.

H COMBINED TACTICS: HEMBRILLO BASIN, APRIL 6–7, 1880

(1) Late afternoon, April 6: Capt Carroll, with Cos D & F, 9th Cavalry, advances into Hembrillo Basin and towards Victorio's camp from the north. Lookouts alert the Apaches in time for them to set a defensive V-shaped ambush from positions on Carroll's Ridge and Apache Ridge; these open fire, blocking Carroll's advance and his access to Rock House Spring. Carroll drives the warriors off the eastern slopes of Carroll's Ridge, but then becomes trapped, and has to form a defensive overnight position.

(2) Victorio's warriors close in around Carroll's command, sniping, and preventing the troopers from fetching water from Rock House Spring. At first light they launch infiltrating attacks, to such close quarters that some troopers have to defend themselves with their revolvers.

(3) At daybreak on April 7, Lt Cusack arrives with Cos A & G, 9th Cavalry, and relieves Carroll's encircled command.

(4) Almost simultaneously, Capt McLellan arrives by another route, with a detachment of 6th Cavalry and two companies of Apache scouts.

(5) Under attack by both Cusack and McLellan, the Apaches fall back to Victorio's Ridge, where they take up rearguard positions.

(6) McLellan's company of 6th Cavalry attacks the left half of Victorio's line, and the Apache scouts push ahead to hook around behind the hostiles' left flank.

(7) Cusack's companies of 9th Cavalry attack the right half of the Apache rearguard line.

(8) After conducting a steady fighting withdrawal to give their dependants time to escape from the camp area, during the late afternoon of April 7 the Apaches break contact and disperse. Some escape north of Geronimo Peak on horseback, but most move southwards and eastwards into the mountains, switching to the tactics of evasion.

Inset: US Cavalry officer on detachment to lead Indian Scouts, with his Apache corporal. Many officers adopted convenient non-regulation dress when in the field; the Scouts – often identified by red headcloths – favored a mixture of their own dress and US Army issue, and were armed with the same Springfield weapons as the soldiers. The contribution of these scouts to the US Army's campaigns was essential to success, and a number of American officers who served with them became skillful frontier fighters.

A faded but interesting photo of a group of Apache scouts with a white or mixed-blood guide and an Army officer. The white man, wearing a slouch hat, has a Winchester carbine; in front of him note one of the Apaches wearing a US Army M1872 dress helmet. The Apaches carry M1873 Springfield infantry rifles, and the officer – who has a flamboyantly non-regulation hat, and fringed leggings – holds a Springfield carbine. A decisive right hook around Victorio's line of resistance in the Hembrillo Basin was made by Apache scouts led by Lts Gatewood and Cruse of the 6th Cavalry. (Courtesy Arizona Historical Society, no. 19841)

In this action we see the combination of ambush, attack and evasion techniques. Despite being taken by surprise the Apaches quickly organized an ambush. When this worked better than expected, they surrounded Carroll's force and harassed them throughout the night, denying them access to water. At first light they launched infiltrating attacks. When suddenly confronted with a large number of reinforcements, the Apaches quickly fell back, fought a rearguard action, and scattered. The speed with which the various Apache groups surrounding Carroll evaluated a rapidly changing situation is also noteworthy.

Finally, it is worth adding that – like Conline the previous day – Carroll was probably lucky that he was pinned down in the late afternoon rather than earlier in the day. By the time the Apaches had positioned themselves more securely around his exposed position, darkness was gathering. Their night-time sniping was unnerving but quite inaccurate; the moon did not rise until approximately 4.30am on April 7, and even then it was little more than a thumbnail, giving little light. Had Carroll been trapped earlier in the day, or had reinforcements not arrived early the following morning, his men and horses would have become sitting targets for the better-positioned Apaches. He would have been faced with the choice of either attempting a break-out, storming one of the surrounding ridges, or digging in to hold out as best he could – short of water, and outnumbered by the rifles of approximately a hundred Apaches, most of them on higher ground.

OTHER ASPECTS OF APACHE WARFARE

The targeting of horses and mules

One of the most effective Apache tactics was their targeting of their enemies' mounts and pack animals. As noted, horses were the primary target in the opening seconds of an ambush. Moreover, the Apaches also killed and crippled hundreds of US Army horses and pack mules by deliberately leading the Cavalry over the roughest terrain imaginable for weeks or even months at a time. The 9th Cavalry – just one of ten US Cavalry regiments – sustained 34.4 percent of the Army's overall losses of horses (died, lost and stolen) between July 1879 and June 1880. The Apache strategy of encouraging the 9th Cavalry to engage in long pursuits produced the situation that in May and June 1880 the regiment had fewer serviceable than unserviceable horses.

The numbers of Army mules died, lost and stolen during the financial years July 1876–June 1881, and the numbers purchased to replace them, also tell an eloquent story:

	1876/77	1877/78	1878/79	1879/80	1880/81
Mules lost	696	781	758	918	687
Bought	842	1,162	1,149	2,265	1,006

These figures make a good argument that Victorio's Apaches were having an appreciable effect upon the US Army's overall supply of mules. The key year is 1879–80, when the only major conflict with American Indians was that with the Apaches in New Mexico. The large numbers of mules purchased in that year may reflect a realization by the US Army that a doubling of the inventory of pack mules was essential for the logistic support of troops engaged in this campaign. Indeed, at the end of May 1880, the equine casualties inflicted both directly and indirectly by the Apaches led General of the Army William T. Sherman to inform Col Edward Hatch (commanding the 9th Cavalry, and the District of New Mexico) that there was no more money available for the purchase of fresh horses and mules until Congress approved the Army's next annual budget.

Mule-packers at work. Mule-trains were essential for keeping US Army detachments supplied in the field during their long pursuits of hostile Apaches, and losses among the Army's mule herd could be a significant drag on operations. (Courtesy Arizona Historical Society, no.19510)

Apache reactions to American technology

The Apaches quickly learned to appreciate the threat of the **telegraph,** and reacted by destroying sections of the wires. This might have the two-fold benefit of hampering US Army communications, while drawing Army attention and personnel to a particular place. In January 1880, when Victorio needed to distract attention from the rustled herd of livestock being driven from the Mexican border to the Mescalero reservation (see above, "Victorio's evasion strategy"), Maj Morrow's attention was attracted in the first place by the destruction of a long section of telegraph line between Fort Cummings and La Mesilla. When repair teams arrived on the scene they reported the discovery of a large trail left by the Apaches, and Morrow set his forces in motion.

Victorio may also have employed a more subtle variation in 1880, and it was certainly known to the US Army in 1885–86. The telegraph wire would be cut at the top of the pole or in any trees through which the line passed, and the two ends would then be tied back in place with strips of rawhide. This obliged the Army's repair teams to take the time to check every pole and tree until they discovered the break.

Examination of the Hembrillo Basin battle site suggests that the Apaches deployed different types of breech-loading **rifles** to maximize their advantages. Winchester and Henry lever-action repeating rifles – with their high rate of fire, but shorter effective ranges – were deployed closer to the US Cavalry positions, while Apaches with Springfield and Remington single-shot rifles were deployed to take advantage of their longer effective range. A number of the ambushes discussed above also show that the Apaches appreciated the value of catching their enemies in a crossfire from well-protected positions surrounding the target; the riflemen would also be sited slightly above the killing-ground, to avoid "friendly fire" from other Apache positions.

The Apaches were also aware of the psychological effect of breech-loading weapons. At the end of April 1880, Victorio's warriors struck the mining and ranching communities along the southern edge of the Mogollon Mts of New Mexico. It was reported that when the Apaches attacked some families who had "forted up" on one ranch near present-day Alma:

> The Indians were able to keep up a constant fire as fifteen warriors would drive up and fire then drop back to reload their guns and another fifteen would take their place thereby keep up [sic] a constant fire as they were always moving in a circle. There were two-hundred thirteen warriors counted.

In truth, this raiding party was probably made up of no more than 25 to 30 warriors, and the attack may have been carried out by as few as ten to 15 men. The Apaches would habitually use the terrain for "fire and movement," giving an exaggerated impression of their numbers. If the enemy did not flee, then the attack would be abandoned, but it might be repeated several times to test the morale of their opponents. What the Apaches were trying to do was to get the besieged party to abandon the ranch so that it could be ransacked in safety. When this failed, a rearguard was left to pin down the defenders of the buildings while the rest of the Apaches moved on to tackle fresh targets.

The deployment of **artillery** – particularly mountain howitzers, which could easily be concealed in wagons, or broken down and transported by

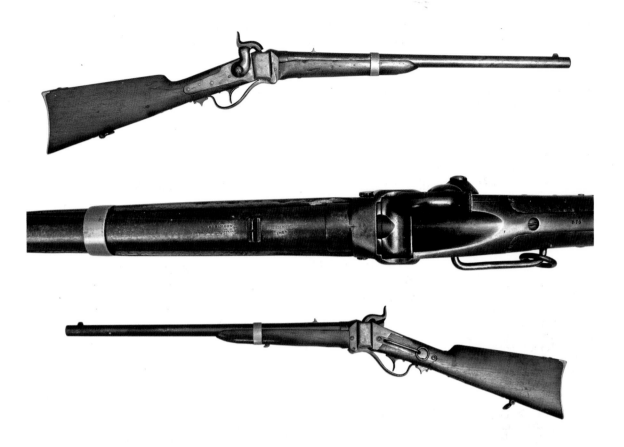

mule – would invariably prompt the Apaches to scatter. Their effect was thus primarily psychological, since by the time these guns were brought into action the Apaches would have had time to break off the engagement. In December 1879, at Fort Marcy, New Mexico, a howitzer was test-fired at a ridge 1,400 yards distant. It was found that with zero elevation the shell range was 300 yards; with 5° and 3° elevation, the shell passed over the target ridge; and the fourth and fifth shots, at 1° elevation, achieved impacts at 550–575 yards' range, though the effectiveness of the shellburst depended upon whether the ground was soft or hard – the best result was a 40-yard radius of fragmentation.

These results suggest that it would take some time to range a howitzer on target, but that once the range was found – and terrain permitting – the weapon had the potential to inflict significant casualties even among concealed and dispersed Apache warriors.

In one skirmish between the 9th Cavalry and Apaches on January 12, 1880 a mountain howitzer was eventually brought into action, and the Apaches withdrew. However, the only man killed in this skirmish was the sergeant directing the deployment of the howitzer – which suggests that the Apaches spotted the threat, tried to counter it, and then withdrew before it could inflict casualties.

The most famous encounter between artillery and Apaches was at the "Battle of Apache Pass" in the Chiricahua Mts on July 14, 1862. Brigadier-General James H. Carleton's volunteer California Column had been organized to counter the Confederate invasion of New Mexico in 1862. An advance party of 140 men of the 1st California Cavalry led by Col

Edward Eyre reached Apache Pass on June 25, and held a parley with Cochise, whose followers had already killed three of Eyre's stragglers. Eyre informed Cochise that he was only passing through, that more troops were camped at Tucson, and that his commander only desired peace with the Apaches. Not realizing that Cochise was at war with the US Army since he had been falsely accused and held in early 1861, Eyre warned the Chiricahua chief that more US troops would be coming west through the pass. More inexplicably, given that Eyre had been ordered to scout the area, he sent no word back to Tucson concerning Apache hostility – even after the discovery of the bodies of his three missing troopers, and after some night-time sniping into Eyre's camp.

The next US troops to enter Apache Pass, three weeks later, were an advance detachment of 60 infantry, eight cavalrymen and two howitzers led by Capt Thomas L. Roberts. He had left Tucson with 102 infantry, 24 troopers, the two howitzers, and 25–30 civilian teamsters. Roberts had detached 13 men to guard a supply dump for following detachments of Carleton's force, and directed 25 soldiers and 20 teamsters to escort his wagons and ration cattle while he moved ahead with the balance of his force towards Apache Pass.

The numbers of Central and Eastern Chiricahuas led by Cochise and Mangas Coloradas are unclear, but they certainly heavily outnumbered Roberts' detachment, and had time to prepare their positions. The soldiers were first ambushed at an abandoned stage station; they had started to relax on arriving there when they were attacked from the rear, and were only able to beat off the Apaches when they deployed the two howitzers. The troops were still several hundred yards from the spring inside Apache Pass; on advancing towards the water, they saw the surrounding ridges well fortified with rock breastworks, from which the concealed Apaches opened a heavy fire. A first attempt to capture the spring, supported by howitzer fire, was driven back. Captain Roberts changed his tactics, and a group of his men led by Sgt Albert Fountain stormed the highest of the ridges. This allowed the rest of the soldiers to seize the spring, while the howitzers were moved to higher ground and shelled the remaining Apache positions. This, combined with the rifle fire of Fountain's men, finally obliged the remaining warriors to withdraw.

The strength of the resistance prompted Roberts to send seven of his cavalrymen back to warn the detachment escorting his wagons and stock. However, this party were seen to be pursued out of the mountains by a large number of Apaches, so, assuming the worst, Roberts decided to return to his supply train himself. There he found that his seven troopers had evaded the Apaches (including Pvt Teal who, unhorsed, had saved himself by wounding Mangas Coloradas). In the meantime the Apaches

Looking eastwards up Diamond Creek in the Black Range/Mimbres Mts of New Mexico. During April–May 1879 Victorio led a number of pursuing US Army detachments over difficult terrain in order to exhaust their horses. On May 29, these Chiricahuas fought a rearguard action against Capt Charles Beyer's 9th Cavalry detachment after leading them up Diamond Creek and over the Black Range to a location that came to be known as Beyer's (or Byer's) Run. (Author's photo)

had re-occupied their positions above the spring in Apache Pass. The next day, Roberts deployed his infantry in a skirmish line across the canyon backed by his cavalrymen, with the two howitzers in the center, and in the event he had little difficulty in driving the warriors from their positions.

Captain Roberts estimated that his men had killed nine Apaches, while he had lost two men killed and two wounded. Both sides agreed that it was the deployment of the howitzers that had been decisive; they had not done much actual damage, but only because the Apaches had chosen to withdraw before they were ranged in on their targets.

Terror tactics

The Apaches had a fearsome reputation for the torturing of captives, and, while certainly exaggerated by their foes, this was not without foundation. One can find lurid tales in the local press, but these stories are, at best, usually second-hand. However, when interviewed by anthropologists and historians in the 1930s–50s the Apaches themselves sometimes acknowledged this reputation. Daklugie, son of Juh, stated that "We had the Sioux beat [for cruelty], especially the Nednhi and Chiricahua. The Warm Springs too. They were brave warriors and real fighting men." [2]

A muzzle-loading Hotchkiss 120mm mountain howitzer, photographed at Fort Bowie. This Napoleonic-looking little cannon, essentially unchanged since the French original appeared in 1827, was light enough to be disassembled and carried into rough terrain in pack-mule loads. Two of these were the decisive factor in the Battle of Apache Pass in July 1862. (Author's photo)

We have noted the deliberate use of cruelty to manipulate white reactions, at Jaralosa in 1879 (see "McEvers Ranch," above). The widespread fear created by such terror tactics could sometimes defeat an opponent before hostilities even commenced; in this sense, inflicting death by torture upon captives fitted in with the Apache principle of minimizing their own casualties.

Dan L. Thrapp (see "Further Reading") argues that the Apache wars with the US can be divided into two phases. The first was the 1860s and early 1870s, when the Apaches were trying to prevent US and Mexican encroachment into their territory; this period ended with the creation of a number of Apache reservations in the Southwest. The second period of warfare, from the mid-1870s to 1886, featured a number of breakouts from these reservations by Apache leaders such as Victorio, Nana, Juh and Geronimo. One suspects that the use of torture was more common in the first period, when it can logically be seen as part of an attempt to warn other potential victims to avoid Apache territory. It seems to have been less prevalent during the second half of the Apache wars, simply because the Apaches often had to move constantly to evade their pursuers, and delaying their movements in order to torture captives only increased their danger of being caught. However, some individual incidents seem well attested, and the reputation for cruelty survived throughout the Apache wars.

2 Juh (pronounced "Whoo") was a leader of the Southern Chiricahua or Nednhi. A successful war leader and contemporary of Victorio and Nana, he had a particular reputation for cruelty.

One of the Apache positions in Apache Pass, seen from the viewpoint of the attacking California Volunteers; this is probably Overlook Ridge, successfully stormed by Sgt Fountain's men. The defensive positions on different features combined to form a horseshoe-shaped line around the spring, which is further up the canyon to the right of this picture. (Author's photo)

Victorio, in particular, has been left with a popular reputation for extreme cruelty that is not generally supported by the primary records (notwithstanding the Jaralosa incident). However, these records do suggest a reason why Victorio's enemies may have labeled him in this way. Whether or not the Apaches used torture, they very rarely took adult males prisoner. Such captives could not be adopted into Apache society, and so were killed if taken alive – and if the Apaches feared detection, they would also kill any women and children who fell into their hands. The warriors fighting under the direction of Victorio and his successor Nana did not draw any European distinctions between combatants and non-combatants, and inflicted very heavy casualties amongst miners, prospectors, sheepherders and ranch hands on both sides of the border between 1879 and 1881. (Indeed, since many of these men would routinely have been armed, the distinction between "combatants" and "non-combatants" was fairly meaningless.)

The treatment suffered at Apache hands depended upon circumstance. James Kaywaykla of the Warm Springs Apaches described an occasion when four Mexicans, including a woman and child, had been killed. Despite his obvious horror when recalling the event many years later, Kaywaykla also pointed out that the Apaches were being closely pursued by US troops, and that any live witnesses could jeopardize their own safety. When Apaches were not feeling threatened they usually would not harm women and children. Kaywaykla recalled an incident when a party led by Nana caught two adolescent boys in New Mexico. Nana ordered his second-in-command, Kaytennae, to get rid of the two captives, as they might alert the authorities to the location of the raiders. However, Kaytennae, as the leader of the rearguard party, chose to release them – a decision that Nana accepted without comment. In this case the Apaches were on the move, and by the time any alarm was raised they would have been far away.

There was even an incident when Nana and his warriors took adult males prisoner and then released them. This occurred at Monica Springs on August 2/3, 1881 when, despite being pursued by a detachment of the 9th Cavalry and Apache scouts, the captives were held while their ranches were ransacked and then released. The reason for this was that most of the men involved were ex-reservation employees with whom Nana had been acquainted in the early 1870s, and with whom – since they survived the experience – he must have enjoyed good relations. Apache warriors, while ruthless, usually had a clear sense of honor.

The fear of hostile Apaches had a far wider effect upon economic activity than was warranted by the losses they actually inflicted. Although Apache raids by small numbers of warriors caused relatively heavy local casualties, these were a fraction of the local population. Yet those who survived would understandably "fort up," and most economic activity by miners, freighters and traders would cease while the threat was perceived to be high.

THE FAILURE OF APACHE RESISTANCE

The three key weaknesses of the Apache guerrillas were the willingness of other Apaches to serve in the US Army as scouts; the difficulty of maintaining a secure supply of rifles and ammunition; and simple lack of numbers – despite the well-documented ability of small war parties to achieve effects out of all proportion to their strength.

Beginning with Gen Crook in 1871–72, US commanders were able to exploit inter-tribal rivalries to enlist hundreds of Apache scouts, whose deployment was usually decisive – particularly their tracking skills. Victorio's only major defeat in US territory was inflicted by 62 Apache scouts led by Capt Henry K. Parker, on May 23/24, 1880, at an unknown location in the Black Range somewhere between present-day Winston and Kingston. During the night the Apache scouts surrounded the camp on three sides, and at daybreak they opened fire. Victorio had stationed a single sentry above his camp, and this man was picked off by one of the Apache scouts while the rest of this group volleyed into the camp. Victorio's followers, completely surprised, attempted to flee; blocked by a second group of scouts, they then tried to escape in another direction, only to be blocked once more by Parker's third group. Finding all avenues of escape cut off, the survivors took refuge among boulders, and a long stalemate ensued. Victorio was wounded in the leg during the attack, and he and his surviving followers were only able to escape when the Apache scouts – almost out of ammunition – had to withdraw, since expected US Army reinforcements failed to materialize. Victorio was reported to have lost 55 of his followers on this occasion, although many of these were women and children.

When Nana launched his famous raid into New Mexico in July and August 1881 he and his men fought a number of skirmishes with US troops. When faced by Army detachments accompanied by Apache scouts the

A group identified as "Crawford's Scouts," so presumably from the battalion of about 100 White Mountain and Chiricahua Apaches of Indian Scout Cos A, B & C that were led into Mexico in January 1886 by Capt Emmet Crawford, in pursuit of Geronimo. Crawford and his chief scout Tom Horn were among seven men wounded – Crawford mortally – when they were fired upon in error by Mexican state troops. Note the blue US Army "sack coats" worn by nearly all these men, some with NCO chevrons, and their long Springfield M1873 infantry rifles. (Courtesy Arizona Historical Society, no. 63674)

hostiles would immediately try to break contact with their pursuers. On three occasions during this expedition Nana's raiders stood their ground and defeated detachments from the 9th Cavalry; none of these three patrols was accompanied by Apache scouts.

General Crook's 1883 Sierra Madre expedition, which persuaded the Apaches to surrender, was only successful because of his predominant use of Apache scouts; the only US troops present were a single company of cavalrymen who acted as escort to the expedition's mule-train. It was the pressure and persuasion applied by Apache scouts, not the deployment of thousands of US troops, which persuaded Chihuahua, Nana, Ulzana, Naiche and Geronimo to surrender in 1886.

* * *

The adoption of modern weapons did allow the evolution of Apache guerrilla tactics into a more aggressive form than the hit-and-run warfare characteristic of the 1860s, but these more aggressive tactics could only be sustained if there were plentiful and secure sources of rifles and ammunition. Such security of supply was rarely, if ever, established, and was a constant source of concern for Apache leaders. The ammunition that could be picked up by raiding was never enough to keep them adequately supplied. They had to engage with illegal traders on both sides of the border in order to replenish their stocks of weapons and cartridges, and – despite their own formidable reputation – the Apaches had to remain vigilant for treachery during such trading sessions. There were a number of occasions when, having concluded their trade in Mexican towns, warriors were persuaded to get drunk with their hosts, and were then killed for the scalp bounty.

A major contributing factor to Victorio's death at Tres Castillos in northern Chihuahua on October 14/15, 1880 was his band's shortage of ammunition due to US Army initiatives. In the immediate aftermath of the Hembrillo Basin battle the Mescalero Apache reservation was placed under close guard by the Army. The attempt to disarm and dismount the Mescaleros was botched, but the effective closing of the reservation shut down Victorio's surest source of ammunition. When he tried to bypass troops in New Mexico by traveling through West Texas in an attempt to reach the Mescalero reservation, he was outmaneuvered by detachments from the 10th Cavalry (then commanded, along with the District of the Pecos, by the famous Civil War hero Col Benjamin H. Grierson). Starved of ammunition, and pursued by Chihuahua state troops led by Col Joaquin Terrazas, assisted by troops from New Mexico led by Col George P. Buell, Victorio had to disperse many of his warriors in search of fresh ammunition. These men were absent when Terrazas trapped Victorio and his remaining followers at Tres Castillos.

* * *

It must be remembered that although Victorio, Nana, Juh, Ulzana, Chihuahua and other Apache leaders sometimes achieved a temporary tactical superiority, they generally had the numbers stacked against them. They very rarely directed more than 150 men against a far more numerous array of forces. In Victorio's case, the Army effort was spearheaded by the 9th Cavalry supported by the 15th Infantry, but by the time he was killed he had also faced strong detachments from the 4th, 6th and 10th Cavalry, with support from the 13th and 16th Infantry regiments. This opposition was intermittently enhanced by civilian volunteers recruited to protect settlements in New Mexico, by Mexican state troops from Chihuahua and Sonora, and – from late 1879 – by occasional Mexican Federal Army operations, such as those led by Gen Geronimo Trevino. In the final pursuit of Geronimo in 1885–86 almost a quarter of the US Army – about 5,000 men – were deployed in the search for fewer than 50 warriors.

Finally, while we have seen that the Apaches were superbly adept guerrillas, they were not perfect. Occasionally they could be caught off their guard, and, given their small numbers, these occasions could have decisive consequences. (In a reversal of a modern comment on counter-terrorist warfare, we might say that the Apaches had to be lucky every time, while the US Army only had to get lucky once or twice.) In his defeat by Apache

The famous photo taken by C.S. Fly of Tombstone at Canyon de los Embudos in Mexico in March 1886, during Gen Crook's negotiations with the hostile Apaches. Geronimo is mounted on the left, Naiche on the right. (Courtesy Arizona Historical Society, no. 7816)

scouts in May 1880, Victorio had camped on a site that turned into a death-trap. He had correctly assumed that he had shaken off the 9th Cavalry, but apparently he had not factored the Apache trackers into the equation, and he suffered the grievous consequences.

One of the most serious defeats inflicted upon Apaches was a consequence of the failure of the advance guard in their standard "marching formation" (as outlined in Plate A). On or about April 18, 1882, some 60 Apaches from the Sierra Madre Mts appeared on the San Carlos reservation, and forced a large number of Warm Springs Apaches under Loco to return with them to Mexico. During their flight they suffered a few losses when an element of the 4th Cavalry caught up with them in Doubtful Canyon on April 23. By April 27 the fugitive Apaches were in Mexico, and, assuming that US troops would not follow them over the border, they halted for a victory celebration on the edge of the Sierra Enmedio. They were unaware that two Apache scout companies backed up by two companies of the 6th Cavalry were closing in on them. The Apache scouts tried to surround the camp, but were discovered prematurely; while suffering some casualties in a fierce fire-fight, the hostiles held off the scouts and troopers and escaped at sundown.

It was as they were fleeing further south on the following day, with one eye over their shoulders for pursuing US troops, that they ran into a force of Mexican soldiers. Apparently the Apache advance guard had passed the Mexican ambush before they spotted it, and then inexplicably failed to alert the main group, comprising mainly women and children. The Mexicans attacked this party, doing fearful execution among the Apache families before the rearguard of warriors arrived. These Apaches held the Mexicans off in a particularly savage battle, but the damage had been done. Shapard estimates that about 400 Apache men, women and children had left San Carlos. By the time the Apaches reached the Sierra Madre over 100 had been killed, and a further 33 women and children had been captured by the Mexicans. Had the Apache advance guard done its job properly, this disaster might have been avoided.

FURTHER READING

There is a large amount of literature on the Apache Wars, but some of the more easily accessible and available material is listed below. The archaeological works by Laumbach *et al* (2001 & 2005) are detailed investigations of two key actions in 1880.

Ball, E., *In the Days of Victorio: Recollections of a Warm Springs Apache* (University of Arizona Press; Tucson, 1970)

Ball, E., *Indeh: An Apache Odyssey* (University of Oklahoma Press; Norman, 1980)

Betzinez, J., *I Fought with Geronimo* (Stackpole, Mechanicsville, 1959; r/p University of Nebraska Press, London, 1987)

Cozzens, P., *Eyewitnesses to the Indian Wars 1865–1890, Vol I: The Struggle for Apacheria* (Stackpole; Mechanicsville, 2001)

Cozzens, P., *Eyewitnesses to the Indian Wars 1865–1890, Vol V: The Army and the Indian* (Stackpole; Mechanicsville, 2005)

Cruse, T., *Apache Days and After* (Caxton Printers Ltd, London, 1941; r/p University of Nebraska Press, London, 1987)

Goodwin, G., *Western Apache Raiding and Warfare* (University of Arizona Press; Tucson, 1998)

Haley, J.L., *Apaches: A History and Culture Portrait* (University of Oklahoma Press, Norman, 1981)

Hook, J., *The Apaches* (Men-at-Arms 186; Osprey, London, 1987)

Laumbach, K.W., *Hembrillo, An Apache Battlefield of the Victorio War: The Archaeology and History of the Hembrillo Battlefield* (Prepared for the White Sands Missile Range, New Mexico by Human Systems Research Inc; 2001)

Laumbach, K.W., D.D. Scott & J. Wakeman, *Conline's Skirmish: An Episode of the Victorio War. Archaeological and Historical Documentation of an 1880s Skirmish Site on White Sands Missile Range* (Prepared for The Directorate of Public Works, White Sands Missile Range, New Mexico, by Human Systems Research Inc; 2005)

Opler, M.E., *An Apache Life-Way: The Economic, Social, & Religious Institutions of the Chiricahua Indians* (University of Chicago Press, 1941; r/p University of Nebraska Press, Lincoln, 1996)

Roberts, D., *Once They Moved Like The Wind: Cochise, Geronimo and the Apache Wars* (Pimlico; London, 1998)

Robinson, S., *Apache Voices: Their Stories of Survival as Told to Eve Ball* (University of New Mexico Press; Albuquerque, 2000)

Shapard, B., *Chief Loco: Apache Peacemaker* (University of Oklahoma Press; Norman, 2010)

Sweeney, E.R., *Cochise: Chiricahua Apache Chief* (University of Oklahoma Press; Norman, 1991)

Sweeney, E.R., *From Cochise to Geronimo: The Chiricahua Apaches 1874–1886* (University of Oklahoma Press; Norman, 2010)

Sweeney, E.R., *Mangas Coloradas: Chief of the Chiricahua Apaches* (University of Oklahoma Press; Norman, 1998)

Thrapp, D.L., *The Conquest of Apacheria* (University of Oklahoma Press; London, 1967)

Thrapp, D.L., *Victorio and the Mimbres Apaches* (University of Oklahoma Press; London, 1974)

Worcester, D.E., *The Apaches: Eagles of the Southwest* (University of Oklahoma Press; Norman, 1979)

An archetypal image of an Apache scout, wearing almost completely Euro-American clothing and holding a Winchester. (Courtesy Arizona Historical Society, no. 35)

INDEX

References to illustrations are shown in **bold**.
Plates are shown with page locators in brackets.